the hamlyn
herb and **spice**
handbook

Arabella Boxer

Publishing Director Laura Bamford

Executive Editor Polly Manguel
Editor Katey Day
Proof-reader Bridget Jones

Creative Director Keith Martin
Designer Vivek Bhatia
Freelance Designer Stephen Poote

Picture Researcher Christine Junemann
Senior Production Controller Katherine Hockley
Indexer Hilary Bird

Photographer Sandra Lane
Home Economist Louise Pickford
Stylist Wei Tang

The Hamlyn Herb and Spice Handbook by Arabella Boxer

First published in 1999 by Hamlyn
an imprint of Octopus Publishing Group Limited
2–4 Heron Quays, London E14 4JP

Design and illustrations copyright © 1999 Octopus Publishing Group Limited
Text copyright © 1999 Arabella Boxer

The text and illustrations in this book have previously appeared in *The Hamlyn
Herb Book* and *The Hamlyn Spice Book*, both by Arabella Boxer.

British Library Cataloguing-in-Publication Data
A catalogue record for this book is available from the British Library

ISBN 0 600 59669 9

Produced by Toppan
Printed in China

Notes
Standard level spoon measurements are used in all recipes.
1 tablespoon = one 15 ml spoon
1 teaspoon = one 5 ml spoon

Both imperial and metric measurements have been given in all recipes.
Use one set of measurements only and not a mixture of both.

Eggs should be medium (size 3) unless otherwise stated.

Ovens should be preheated to the specified temperature
– if using a fan assisted oven, follow the manufacturer's instructions
for adjusting the time and temperature.

contents

introduction

When I first started writing about herbs in 1980, fresh herbs were hard to find unless you had your own garden, as I did in those days. In the country the village shop might have a bunch of curly parsley or mint when new potatoes and green peas were on sale, but little else. Dried herbs were considered a perfectly good substitute for the real thing, and every kitchen had a shelf jammed full of small glass jars, way past their sell-by date – except such a thing did not exist then. In the city you fared better, but only just. A few speciality food shops sold three or four varieties of fresh herbs during their short season, after which you were reduced to using dried herbs or going without.

People's reactions to herbs, both in general and specific terms, can be quite extreme and totally unpredictable. I find my own tastes have changed radically over the years. Sometimes my initial dislike sprang from a failure to understand the herb in question and how it should be used. Trying to eat savory raw was a case in point. Both sage and rosemary were anathema to me for years, just as they were to Elizabeth David, as she recounts in *Spices, Salts and Aromatics in the English Kitchen* (Penguin, 1970). Now, however, I have changed my mind, largely because I have learnt to use them in ways that give me pleasure: sprigs of rosemary used with garlic in dishes of fried and roast potatoes, and whole leaves of sage fried and scattered over pasta or grilled vegetables. One herb that seems to me strangely under-used is dill, despite the growing popularity of gravadlax. Another neglected herb is

chervil, which has long been one of my favourites.

With the growing emphasis on salads in our diet, salad leaves have once again acquired huge importance. I say 'once again', as we must not forget that in the seventeenth century salads were considered vital. John Evelyn's 'Salad Calendar', published in 1699 in his *Acetaria*, lists no less than thirty-eight different salad leaves and herbs. These include rocket, purslane, sorrel, corn salad, chicory, endive, mustard and cress, and six kinds of lettuce, as well as fennel, chives, sage, balm, tarragon, chervil and mint. How strange it seems that only twenty years ago the eminent food writer Jane Grigson was bemoaning the fact that so many of these excellent plants had been all but forgotten. Now many of them seem to have made a speedy and unexpected comeback. Yet with such extremes of fashion there is always the danger that the food in question may be overused and fall out of favour again. Already sorrel seems to have suffered this fate, for it is no longer as popular as it was in 1970, while basil and rocket may well follow suit, having been over-promoted by misguided chefs.

We tend to think of spices as food flavourings, but in earlier times their uses were manifold. Some, like aniseed and fennel, were used as medicaments in the form of infusions, decoctions and poultices; others, like turmeric, as dyes, or, like cinnamon, cloves and liquorice, as incense; still others, like ginger and saffron, were used in baths, or, like myrrh and sesame seeds, in cosmetics. Similarly, in those days the understanding of what could be used to flavour food was broader and more complex than it is in many cultures today.

In the eighth century, on his death, the Venerable Bede left to his fellow monks his collection of spices, which included aniseed, cinnamon, cloves, cumin, cardamom, galangal, ginger and liquorice. In addition to these there were others whose names mean little to us now: gromic, pelletour, eryngo, gelofrus and sucket. By the fifteenth century we find mention of other spices: saffron, sandalwood (called sanders), mace and mustard. In the seventeenth century, after the formation of the East India Company, we read of pine nuts, candied citrus peel and pickled broom buds being put to use in the kitchen.

Sadly, the traditions of multiple spicing and seasoning have long been forgotten in many Western cuisines. For the past century people have tended to separate different ingredients into categories, and fairly narrow ones at that. Even within the context of food, spices have been denied their individual flexibility, wherein lies much of their appeal. The use of nutmeg, for instance, has been limited to little more than flavouring bread sauce or sprinkling over a junket, while a combination of cinnamon, nutmeg and cloves, called 'pudding spice' or simply 'mixed spice', has been considered adequate for every sweet dish. Likewise, a commercially produced curry powder was thought to be all that was required to reproduce a series of Indian dishes.

At the other end of the scale is the scene in a typical Indian kitchen, where much of each day is spent preparing spices, and where a mixture of different spices are roasted and ground for every dish. At least, that is how it used to be, and still is in rural areas, but in the cities, more and more people are enlisting the aid of food processors and spice mills, and even resorting to buying their spice mixtures ready-made.

Since the end of World War II a growing enthusiasm for international cuisine has spread unabated. But this is confined largely to restaurant meals and the purchase of packaged, ready-to-eat dishes for reheating in the microwave. Thus chicken tikka masala, sweet-and-sour pork and chilli con carne may have almost reached the status of national dishes while being freshly cooked in only a small number of our own kitchens. Many manufacturers now produce jars of cook-in sauces, cans of spiced beans and bottles of salsa. These are bland approximations of the real thing; they may not be bad as far as they go, but they share that dreaded sameness that characterizes packaged foods. How much better, and more enjoyable, to buy the herbs and spices, for these never change, and from these cook something yourself. It's more rewarding certainly, as well as cheaper, healthier and more welcoming.

herb directory
8–49

spring onions *cepa*

Spring onions are also called salad onions and green onions. In Ireland and in the United States they are called scallions, just as they were in Elizabethan England.

Spring onions are not a species in their own right; they are simply the immature form of any number of varieties. This explains why they differ so widely in shape; some are like the Kate Moss of the vegetable world, while others resemble Dolly Parton. Certain varieties of onion, like White Lisbon, are more suited to eating at an early stage than others. The Welsh onion, *Allium fistulosum*, with hollow leaves, is widely cultivated for sale as a spring onion, while in California the immature form of a red onion is used in this fashion, which makes a delightful garnish for a dish of grilled vegetables.

Until quite recently, spring onions were only eaten raw in most Western countries. They are still served raw with many dishes, but with the growing fondness for Eastern food they are now being cooked as well. Many people find them too potent to eat raw, like Irma Rombauer who wrote of the spring onion in her classic American cookbook *Joy of Cooking*: 'The leaf is good as a soup flavouring, the white flesh is often braised, and they are eaten raw by self-assertive people...'.

Spring onions form an inseparable part of the small group of flavourings we associate with stir-frying; the others being garlic, ginger, chillies and coriander. They are also delicious steamed whole, or grilled.

Cultivation

Spring onions are grown from seed, never from sets. The seed should be sown in spring, in fine well-drained garden soil, in partial shade. Welsh onions are especially easy to grow and can be propagated by dividing the clumps in spring, and replanting 30 cm (12 inches) apart. Some may be lifted and used as spring onions while the rest are left to mature. In this way they may be dug as needed all through the year.

Medicinal

Onions were used for medicinal purposes in ancient times by the Egyptians and Persians, Greeks and Romans. They act as a natural antiseptic, antiscorbutic, diuretic and a stimulant to the digestive system. They are often eaten on a regular daily basis to ward off colds and flu.

recipes using spring onions, see pages: 116; 121; 129; 144; 145; 150; 153; 159; 190; 196

garlic

Garlic grew first in Central Asia and has been used both as a flavouring agent for food and as a medicament since ancient times, most notably in ancient Egypt. It is now grown throughout the world, but most prolifically in Asia, California and in the Mediterranean countries, especially in southwest France and Provence, where special garlic fairs and markets are held during the summer. Although garlic was known in Britain in Elizabethan times, it fell into disuse until after World War II, when the writings of Elizabeth David brought it back into favour. There are many different varieties: the two types most popular in France are the white garlic, which is harvested there in June, and the pink, which is lifted in July.

Garlic is a perennial bulb, a member of the onion family. The edible part is the bulb, which grows underground and can be divided into cloves. These are usually peeled before use, then crushed or chopped and fried in oil. Unpeeled cloves may be roasted whole, around a bird for instance, then squashed into a purée. Raw garlic is fairly pungent, but effective when used in moderation, as in the Tuscan bruschetta. Here a thick slice of country bread is grilled, then rubbed with a cut clove of garlic and drizzled with olive oil.

Dried garlic is available throughout the year. The freshest garlic, which is delicious, with large, mild, juicy cloves, is best bought in early summer, directly after its harvest.

Cultivation

Garlic is easy to grow at home. The cloves should be planted 3 cm (1¼ inches) deep and 10 cm (4 inches) apart in light, well-drained soil, in late winter or early spring. When the leaves die back in summer, the garlic can be lifted and hung up in a cool, airy place to dry.

Medicinal

Garlic has a multitude of beneficial effects on health: it is a natural antiseptic and antibiotic, it stimulates the digestive system, it lowers the blood pressure, and it is believed to regulate the level of cholesterol in the bloodstream.

recipes using garlic, see pages: 96; 97 ; 101; 105; 116; 121; 124; 127; 130; 132; 133; 135; 146; 149; 157; 180; 184; 186; 187; 189; 192; 194; 195

chives Allium
schoenoprasum

Chives are a member of the onion family, and grow wild in Britain, Europe, Asia and the United States. They are easily grown in the garden, or even in pots on the windowsill. The flavour of chives is a fugitive and elusive one, for their essential oil is highly volatile. For this reason they are best used in cold dishes, like vichyssoise, salsa verde and potato salad. When used in hot dishes, like chive sauce for boiled beef or consommé, they should be added only after the cooking is terminated. They contribute a delicious sharp, fresh, green flavour that makes a marvellous foil to pale, bland, creamy dishes.

Cultivation

Chives are perennial and may be grown from seed sown in spring, then thinned out to a distance of 30 cm (12 inches) apart. Germination is slow, so once established it is easier to increase a bed by dividing plants in spring or autumn and replanting them into small clumps about 23 cm (9 inches) apart.

Medicinal

Chives have important medicinal qualities, although their efficacy is less than that of the other, stronger-smelling members of the *Allium* family. None the less, they stimulate the appetite and aid the digestion, act as a gentle laxative and a mild sedative, and contain some iron and vitamin C.

Above: from left, garlic chives and common chives

recipes using chives, see pages: 92; 103; 110; 192

dill

Anethum graveolens

Dill is an annual, a native of continental Europe, which grows up to 60 cm (2 feet) high, with hollow stems, very thin, thread-like leaves and umbels of yellow flowers. The seeds look very like caraway seeds, while the whole plant is so similar to fennel as to be almost indistinguishable from it.

Dill has become one of my favourite herbs in recent years. It was not until I had been to Denmark twice that I learnt to appreciate it, for the Scandinavians use it constantly and to great effect with fish, particularly salmon which they pickle with a mixture of salt, sugar and vast quantities of dill. They serve whole stems of dill wreathed around plain boiled or steamed potatoes to accompany fish. Dill is also popular mixed with soured cream, served with crayfish, prawns and shrimps. In Poland and other parts of Central Europe dill is much used, often with soured cream, in soups, sauces, salads, vegetable dishes and pickles. Dill pickles are small cucumbers preserved in vinegar and flavoured with dill; these are the traditional accompaniment to salt beef sandwiches. In the United States the terms dill seed and dill weed (the leaves) are used to distinguish between the two useful parts of the herb.

Cultivation

Dill is easily grown from seed sown in spring, in drills 25 cm (10 inches) apart, then thinned out to 20 cm (8 inches) between plants. It should not be transplanted as this causes plants to flower, when it is no more use as a herb for its strength goes into woody stems.

Medicinal

Dill has been used since ancient times for both its magical powers and its medicinal properties. It combines the virtues of a stimulant and a sedative, and is both aromatic and carminative (see dill seeds, page 52).

recipes using dill, see pages: 120; 129; 146; 182; 192; 194

camomile Anthemis nobilis, Chamaemelum nobile

Camomile, or chamomile, is a low-growing perennial that has been used for centuries for making paths or small lawns in herb gardens. Its name derives from the Greek *khamaimelon*, meaning 'earth-apple', a reference to the aroma of the leaves and flowers, which is released at the slightest touch. Camomile seems to grow best when walked on.

Cultivation

Camomile may be grown from seed sown in spring, or propagated by dividing the roots into small clumps and replanting 20 cm (8 inches) apart. It needs a light dry soil and plenty of sunlight. If grown in the shade, the plants grow leggy as they reach for the light. The small white daisy-like flowers are borne in early summer, and should be picked when fully open and then dried in the shade.

Medicinal

The flowers are used mainly for making infusions and have various medicinal properties: digestive, febrifugal and calming. They are also used in cosmetics as a rinse for fair hair.

recipe using camomile, see page 200

chervil

I believe that this is currently the most underrated of herbs, yet I cannot help wishing that it might remain so, thus escaping the fate of the over-exposed basil and rocket.

Chervil first grew in the Middle East and southern Russia, and was probably introduced to many European countries by the Romans. It is a biennial, growing about 40 cm (16 inches) tall, with feathery fern-like leaves, small white flowers, and strange little black seed pods. There is also a curly-leafed form, which is especially pretty for using as a garnish, but I think that all chervil is as decorative as it is delicious.

The essential oil of chervil is one of the most fugitive, and it should never be subjected to extreme heat. The leaf is best treated as a garnish, and in the case of hot dishes it should be added after the cooking is over, shortly before serving. It is utterly delicious in delicate consommés, with poached chicken or fish, in a cream sauce, with rice, potatoes and most cooked vegetables, and in lettuce salads. It also forms part of the classic *fines herbes* mixture, along with tarragon, parsley and chives. The *omelette fines herbes* made with this combination, is one of the great egg dishes of all time.

Cultivation

Chervil should be grown from seed, scattered or sown in drills, any time between spring and the end of summer. It can then be thinned out to 20 cm (8 inches) apart. Chervil needs plenty of water but not too much sun; a cool northern bed kept moist with frequent watering is ideal. The best time to use chervil is before it flowers. Like most herbs, chervil loses much of its flavour after it has flowered, even if the flower heads are removed before the seeds have formed.

Medicinal

Chervil is rich in vitamin C, iron, magnesium and carotene. When drunk in the form of raw juice (somewhat unpalatable, alas) or as an infusion, it cleanses the blood, acts as a diuretic and benefits the liver. It is good for treating gout, rheumatism, and eye troubles.

recipes using chervil, see pages: 98; 104; 129; 133; 145; 146; 162; 182; 192

celery leaves — *Apium graveolens*

Although celery may not be generally thought of as a herb, it deserves a place in the herb garden, if only for the sake of its leaves. In some countries a variety of celery is grown specially for its leaves, while in many others celery is sold with all its leaves on, rather than trimmed. The Belgian dish of *anguilles au vert* (eels in green sauce) depends almost entirely for its flavour on large handfuls of celery leaves. Some time ago, on the Greek island of Lesbos, I bought bunches of celery leaves under the impression that they were flat-leaf parsley; they were the only fresh herb to be found on the island at that time.

Celery leaves have a fresh sappy flavour, similar to lovage but less coarse. Like lovage, they can be cooked for long periods with no loss of flavour. A celery stalk forms part of the traditional bouquet garni, with bay leaf, thyme and parsley stalks tucked within it. The crushed seeds are mixed with sea salt to make celery salt for serving with gulls' eggs during their short season.

In medieval times celery grew wild in Britain and still does so today in parts of North and South America. A cultivated form was developed by French and Italian gardeners in the seventeenth century and was imported into England. Smallage was the old-fashioned name for wild celery, which was much used in the past as a pot herb, like parsley.

There are two basic forms of cultivated celery – blanched, or white, and unblanched, or green. The white variety is often preferred for eating raw, as it is less bitter than the green. It used to be hard to grow, but now there is a self-blanching variety that is much simpler.

Cultivation

Celery is a biennial. During its second year it produces flowers and seeds, but is of no further use as a vegetable or herb. It is a winter vegetable, in season from autumn to spring. It is best sown under glass, then planted out when the seedlings are a few centimetres high. The turnip-rooted variety, called celeriac, also produces leaves that can be used as a herb, although in less abundance than true celery.

Medicinal

Celery leaves are composed mainly of cellulose and water, it has few calories while supplying valuable fibre and vitamin C. It is a general tonic for the system, particularly for the nerves and for nervous stomachs. It also acts as a diuretic, laxative and carminative.

recipes using celery leaves see pages: 92; 118; 137

tarragon

Artemisia dracunculus

French tarragon comes from southern Europe and likes to grow in a warm, dry climate. It is semi-hardy and may need some protection from frost. A bushy perennial shrub, it grows 75–90 cm (2½–3 feet) high, with narrow tapering leaves and small white flowers in summer. The flavour varies from plant to plant, like mint.

An understandable confusion exists between French tarragon (*Artemisia dracunculus*) and Russian tarragon (*A. dracunculoides*). Although they are almost identical in appearance, the difference can soon be ascertained by tasting a leaf: whereas the true French tarragon has a strong, clear scent and flavour, the inferior Russian variety has virtually no taste at all, just a faint muddy hint.

Tarragon has been part of the classic French cuisine for hundreds of years and is one of the few herbs that has never fallen out of favour. It has a special affinity with chicken, eggs, salads and cream sauces, and makes one of the best of all flavoured vinegars. Much of its appeal derives from its delicacy; and it is easy to see that its essential oil is a volatile one. Yet it will withstand short periods of cooking.

Cultivation

French tarragon can rarely be grown from seed and the best way is by taking cuttings or transplanting a root. (Russian tarragon is easily grown from seed, but does not deserve garden space.) Plant cuttings 30 cm (12 inches) apart in good soil, in a sunny spot. Feed them during the growing period, then cut them down to ground level in autumn and cover the plants with straw or bracken. Replant in a fresh spot every year.

Medicinal

Like many other herbs, tarragon acts as a stimulant and a calming agent at the same time. While it stimulates the appetite, the kidneys and the bladder, it calms attacks of indigestion, flatulence and hiccups. It acts on the system as a general tonic as well as a diuretic, laxative and vermifuge.

recipes using tarragon, see pages: 129; 145; 146; 182; 192

borage Borago officinalis

Borage is a showy plant, which adds interest and appeal to the herb garden. It is a hardy annual, very easy to grow, reaching about 50 cm (18 inches) high. It has large pale green, hairy leaves and small, bright blue star-shaped flowers.

Its most common use is as a decoration for Pimms and other wine- or fruit-based drinks. Whole sprigs, complete with leaves and flowers, are immersed in the drink, which is served in a large glass jug. Both leaves and flowers give a faint cucumber-like flavour. The flowers are sometimes crystallized for decorating iced cakes, and the leaves and flowers may be eaten raw in salads.

Cultivation

Borage is easily grown from seed, which may be sown either in autumn or spring. Autumn-sown crops will flower in late spring, while those sown in spring should bloom in summer. (This is preferable, for its uses are related to midsummer.) Borage may also be propagated by taking cuttings.

Medicinal

In the Middle Ages borage was believed to dispel melancholy and promote courage, and to possess restorative powers. It is rich in calcium and potassium, and acts as a diuretic by helping to stimulate sluggish kidneys. The leaves may be made into an infusion, to be drunk hot to relieve catarrh, or at any temperature to combat stress.

mizuna

Brassica rapa var. japonica

According to Joy Larkcom in *Oriental Vegetables* (John Murray, 1991), her classic book on the subject, mizuna is a plant of Chinese origin that has been cultivated for centuries in Japan. I first encountered it in California in 1987, where it was as popular as rocket is today. Now it is gradually starting to make its appearance elsewhere. Although it may not yet be widely available in shops or supermarkets, it is being cultivated by enterprising growers for avant-garde restaurants and for particular ethnic communities.

Cultivation

Mizuna is easy to grow, being remarkably hardy and slow to bolt. It may be sown out of doors from late spring to early autumn. (Its season may be extended from early spring to late autumn by the use of cloches.) Some two to three weeks after sowing, the seedlings will be ready for transplanting; this should be done so that they are 10–25 cm (4–10 inches) apart, depending on whether you want small or large plants. Mizuna can also be grown throughout the winter in an unheated greenhouse, and provides an extremely valuable winter salad.

marigold Calendula officinalis

The marigold originated in southern Europe and has been cultivated in Britain for hundreds of years; it was always included in medieval herb gardens. Cultivated throughout the world, the marigold is a hardy annual growing about 30 cm (12 inches) high. It closes up its petals at dusk and opens them again at sunrise. It is mentioned in *The Winter's Tale* accordingly: 'The marigold that goes to bed wi' the sun, and with him rises weeping.'

The marigold has been popular as a pot herb, as a cheap substitute for saffron, and as a way of introducing colour into what were often dull-looking dishes. In the past it was used not just for sweet dishes, but also for meat and fish. The petals, usually dried, were strewn over a soup, a beef stew or a salad. They were also used with fish and rice, and in sweets, like egg custard, cakes and biscuits.

Cultivation

Marigolds are best grown from seed sown in spring. The plants should be thinned out to 30 cm (12 inches) apart, enabling them to spread. They thrive in a light rich soil, in a sunny position. If some of the flower heads are left on the plants after flowering, they will seed themselves the following year. To dry marigolds, simply lay the flower heads on sheets of paper and dry quickly in an airy place out of the sun. Once they have dried, rub off the petals and store them in airtight jars.

Medicinal

The marigold was formerly used for treating bronchial problems and for bathing the eyes. It is now used in lotions for chapped skin.

recipe using marigold, see page 162

curry leaves

Chalcas koenigii, Murraya koenigii

There is much confusion between curry leaves (*Chalcas koenigii*), the curry plant (*Helichrysum italicum*), and daun salaam (*Eugenia polyantha*). Curry leaves are small, glossy evergreen leaves, much like small bay leaves in appearance. They are borne on a decorative tree, a native of South-east Asia, and they give off a delicious Eastern fragrance in the breeze. The leaves are best used fresh, though it is hard to buy them in this state in the West; the dried leaves have less flavour. Curry leaves are one of the ingredients of commercially made curry powders, and are also used in the home to make curries and similar dishes. They may be chopped or crumbled, then fried in oil at the start of a dish, before adding the spices, or added at the end of cooking, after frying with spices. Dried leaves may also be ground to a powder or made into a paste for flavouring curries and other dishes. Their flavour combines well with garlic, ginger, chillies and fresh coriander.

The curry plant is entirely different: a low-growing herbaceous plant with silvery-green spiky leaves and yellow flowers. Although it is a pretty plant to include in the herb garden, space permitting, it is of no use in the kitchen, despite the fact that its leaves emit a pleasant smell of curry when crushed.

Daun salaam is a highly aromatic evergreen leaf much used in Indonesian cooking. It is very similar to the curry leaf both in appearance and in flavour. It is best used fresh.

Cultivation

The tree that bears the curry leaf we are concerned with is easy to grow and small enough to include in the garden, but it is not often found in nurseries outside Asia.

Medicinal

In India the bark, leaves and root are used as a tonic.

recipe using curry leaves, see page 130

coriander leaves

Coriandrum sativum

A native of the eastern Mediterranean, coriander is mentioned in the Bible, and seeds have been found in ancient Egyptian tombs. It was brought to northern Europe by the Romans, who used it as a flavouring, a preservative and a medicament. In 1492 it was taken by Columbus to the Caribbean and from there it reached the Latin American countries. Almost indistinguishable from flat parsley, coriander grows to about 60 cm (2 feet) tall. All parts of the plant are edible and today it is used throughout the world.

Both individuals and countries react to coriander in quite extreme ways. Few people are dispassionate about it: they either love it or hate it. It is much loved, for example, in all the Latin American countries, the Caribbean, India and China, but not in Japan. It is widely used in North Africa and the Middle East, but not on the northern shore of the Mediterranean. It is not known in Spain, yet it is much liked in Portugal. It is probably in South-east Asia that it is most appreciated. In Indonesia the seeds alone are used, while in neighbouring Thailand both leaves and root are used as flavouring. The fresh coriander leaf goes well with garlic, chillies, ginger, spring onions and tomatoes. It lends its character to fresh, hot, vibrant dishes, and complements chicken, fish and vegetables. Mexican dishes, like guacamole and salsa, could not be made without it.

Cultivation

Coriander is easy to grow, given certain conditions. It needs a light well-drained soil, plenty of moisture and sun. It should be sown in early spring, once all danger of frost is past. When it has flowered, the leaves alter their character and their flavour deteriorates. Unless you wish it to self-seed, this is the time to dig it up.

Medicinal

Coriander was used as a medicament by the ancient Greeks and Romans. It combines the effects of a sedative and a stimulant, and can become addictive if abused. The seeds may be chewed as a digestive or diuretic, while both the leaves and seeds can be used to make an infusion.

recipes using coriander leaves, see pages: 97; 107; 116; 118; 124; 130; 132; 150; 185; 190; 192; 195; 196

lemon grass

Lemon grass is a native of South-east Asia, where it is highly valued, since lemons do not grow in tropical climates. Like coriander, lemon grass is one of those exotic herbs that only recently became widely available.

Lemon grass is a curious plant, like a cross between a root vegetable and a grass. The part that we use as a flavouring is the bottom section of the swollen leaf stem, just above the root. It is very hard indeed, and should be crushed before use. In most cases it is removed before the dish is eaten, having served its purpose, but in some cases, as in a stir-fry, it needs to be eaten in the dish. In this case, only the very tender inner parts should be used, and they should be finely sliced, chopped or grated beforehand. When fresh lemon grass is not available, a dried form called *sereh* can be bought in Indonesian food shops.

Like lemon balm and lemon verbena, lemon grass contains one of the components of the lemon, oil of lemon, without the other, citric lemon acid. So it possesses the fragrant lemony quality of the lemon without its tart, zingy character. Therefore, as a fresh substitute, use lemon balm, lemon verbena or lemon zest.

Lemon grass is usually used in combination with garlic, ginger, chillies and coriander, to enhance spiced dishes of fish, chicken and noodles, soups and salads.

Cultivation

A fresh root of lemon grass may be potted up and grown under glass or as a houseplant. Alternatively, it may be grown in a pot out of doors during the summer, then moved inside for the colder months.

Medicinal

The crushed stalk is sometimes used in an infusion as a sedative and to relieve colic. It can be used with lovage and geranium leaves to make a cleansing bath for oily skin.

recipes using lemon grass, see pages: 115; 116; 133; 189

rocket
Eruca sativa

Rocket originated in southern Europe. It has always been popular in France, where it is called *roquette*, and in Italy, where it is known as *rucola*, as well as in Turkey, the Middle East, and the United States, where it is called arugula. It was introduced to Britain in the sixteenth century and was a popular kitchen herb in Elizabethan and Stuart times, eaten raw in salads, like land cress, watercress, and mustard. Although naturalized by the mid-seventeenth century – after the Great Fire of London in 1666 rocket spread rapidly through the ruins – it was later forgotten and did not regain its culinary position until the early 1980s.

The leaves have a delicious peppery flavour and can be eaten alone or mixed with other green leaves. The wild leaf has a much stronger flavour; the cultivated leaf is larger, milder and less bitter.

Cultivation

Rocket is easily grown at home by sowing seed in the open in spring. It must be watered regularly or it will become rank and sour. Frequent picking encourages new growth.

Medicinal

Rocket is a recognized antiscorbutic, and was formerly used for this purpose and as a tonic and a mild stimulant. For medicinal purposes, the plant is at its most effective when gathered while it is still in flower.

recipes using rocket, see pages: 104; 142; 165; 166; 184

fennel

Fennel grew wild in southern Europe, around the shores of the Mediterranean, and later became naturalized around the coastline of Britain. There are three main varieties: wild fennel (*Foeniculum vulgare*), common garden fennel (*F. officinale*), and Florence fennel (*F. dulce*). The first is grown mainly for the sake of its seeds and its leaves, while the others are cultivated for use as a vegetable.

Fennel can be treated as a herb, as it traditionally was in England – the leaves chopped and added to a sauce for fish – or as a vegetable, as it is in France and Italy: eaten raw, thinly sliced, as a salad, or braised and served as a hot vegetable. In Provence dried fennel stalks are thrown on the fire before grilling fish over the open flames. In Italy raw fennel stalks used to be eaten at the end of a meal, like celery – but without the cheese – as a digestive.

Cultivation

Fennel is easily grown, requiring little more than some well-drained soil and a sunny position. It also needs plenty of room if it is not to swamp the other plants, for it grows about 1.5 m (5 feet) tall. It can be propagated either by seed or by root division. If sown, the seeds should be placed in drills 40 cm (15 inches) apart, and later transplanted. In its pattern of growth fennel is very similar to dill and caraway, with hollow, woody stems, umbels of yellow flowers, small, oval, finely-divided leaves and small, oval seeds. Once cut, the leaves are almost indistinguishable from dill; the two plants should not be grown in close proximity or they will cross-pollinate.

Medicinal

Fennel has been much valued for its therapeutic properties for hundreds of years as a spring cure, an antidote to wind, a diuretic, tonic, sedative and a cure for failing eyesight. The roots, leaves and seeds have generally been used in poultices, infusions and baths for eyes, hands and feet.

recipe using fennel, see page 101

hops Humulus lupulus

Before they were cultivated, hops grew wild in Britain, continental Europe and North America. The young shoots are much prized in Belgium, Germany and parts of northern France, and the wild hop shoots are considered a delicacy in Venice. They may be cooked like asparagus, in lightly salted boiling water, then served on toast with melted butter, or with poached or scrambled eggs. The first time I ate them was in Brussels, where they are called *jets d'houblon*, and I thought them quite wonderful. They also make an excellent risotto, as is done in Venice with the wild hop shoots (called *bruscandoli*) during their short season in early May.

It is almost impossible to get hold of hop shoots that have not been sprayed, which is all the more reason for growing one's own. Hops are extraordinarily decorative plants, and they come in two forms: green and golden. They are climbers, very similar to vines, with pretty pale yellowish-green cones. These are the female flowers, and contain the resin that gives the hop its distinctive smell and flavour. At Hardwick Hall, the romantic Elizabethan mansion in Derbyshire built by Bess of Hardwick, one of the most striking decorative features of the herb garden is the arrangement of alternating pillars of green and golden hops, trained over tripods of tall poles, rising out of herb beds. Hardwick was built only some fifty years after the first imports of hops came from the Continent, in the first half of the sixteenth century, and the introduction of 'hopped' ale. (The use of hops in beer-making gave this beverage a new flavour and doubled its keeping qualities.)

Cultivation

Hops are perennials and are easy to grow so long as they are given some support. Although they die down to ground level each winter, the new shoots will grow roughly 6–7.5 m(18–25 feet) each year. Hops can be grown from seed sown out of doors in early spring, then thinned out to 15–30 cm (6–12 inches) apart. The plants can be increased by root division, also in spring. The young shoots should always be thinned out in the spring.

Medicinal

Hops were viewed with mistrust for centuries, believed to induce melancholy. Yet they have accepted powers, especially as a tonic for the nerves, being both sedative and soporific. They also act as a diuretic and can calm pain. For medicinal uses, only female flowers are used, both fresh and dried.

bay leaves

The bay tree has been growing wild around the shores of the Mediterranean since ancient times. It was believed to possess magical powers against witchcraft and disease, and came to symbolize excellence. For this reason the Greeks and Romans wove its branches into wreaths with which to crown their victors.

Bay leaves are not a true herb, since the bay tree grows up to 18 m (60 feet) high, yet, being highly aromatic, they have always been treated as such. They form part of the classic bouquet garni along with parsley and thyme, and are used to flavour fish stocks and court-bouillons, meat stocks and soups, terrines and casseroles. They require long, slow cooking to bring out their flavour, and may be used equally well plucked fresh off the tree or dried. They are very potent and should be used with caution. The dried leaves are quite tough, so it is best to use them whole in cooking and to remove them before serving.

The bay tree is rarely allowed to grow to its full height; it is more frequently seen as a bushy shrub or a small tree grown in a pot or tub and trimmed into a decorative shape. It is a handsome plant, with its glossy, dark evergreen leaves, its yellowish flowers, and the small black berries that follow.

Cultivation

The bay tree is simple to cultivate, for it grows well in any garden soil and likes the sun. It does equally well in tubs or large pots and in open ground. Additional bushes can be grown from cuttings taken in spring or autumn.

Medicinal

Bay leaves have some medicinal uses – an infusion helps to stimulate appetite and aids digestion, while rubbing with bay oil eases muscular aches and pains – but it is in the kitchen that they are most valuable.

recipes using bay leaves, see pages: 96; 137; 166; 185; 194

lavender Lavandula angustifolia

Lavender is an evergreen perennial shrub, low-growing and bushy in shape, with silvery-grey leaves and spikes of flowers in mauve, light blue, purple or white. *Lavandula angustifolia*, commonly known as English lavender, grows about 1 m (3 feet) high, with light blue flowers, making a handsome hedge; there is also a dwarf variety, which is useful for edging beds of herbs or flowers.

In medieval times lavender was much used as a strewing herb and was almost always included in herb gardens. I have seen it still used for strewing today, when spending Easter on the Greek isle of Patmos some years ago. Here wild lavender is spread thickly over the streets before the holy procession is due to pass and in the square where the Easter ceremonies are held.

In Tudor times, lavender was used for scenting linen, for medicinal purposes and, to a lesser degree, in food, to flavour honey, creams and jellies; little twigs of peeled lavender were also employed to spear sweetmeats. Today lavender is used mainly in making lavender water and essential oil, and in scented pillows, sachets and pot-pourri. It can also be put to good use in the kitchen: to flavour custards and ice creams, and to add its inimitable flavour to jams and jellies.

Cultivation

Lavender can be grown from seed or from cuttings. Cuttings should be about 7 cm (3 inches) long and planted in a sandy compost. If this is done in late summer or early autumn, in a cold frame or under a cloche, the cuttings will be ready for planting out the following spring. Lavender needs a well-drained sandy soil in an open sunny position.

Medicinal

Lavender has myriad medicinal uses, as a diuretic, for calming nervous disorders of the stomach and as an inhalant for asthma.

recipe using lavender, see page 154

lovage

Levisticum officinale

Lovage is a native of the Mediterranean region and, like so many plants, was probably spread through Europe by the Romans. It now grows wild near the sea in north-east England and in the north-eastern United States; a related variety, Scottish Lovage (*Levisticum scoticum*), can be found growing on rocky coasts in Scotland. It is a vigorous plant which can grow over 1.8 m (6 feet) high. The leaves are deeply indented, similar to those of celery, which they also resemble in flavour. It has yellow flowers borne in umbels. If you have room for it in your garden (preferably in a corner near the back), it is worth including, for it is a handsome plant.

In former times all parts of the plant were eaten: the stems and roots were boiled and eaten as a vegetable, the leaves used as a pot herb, and the seeds used in baking, like caraway seeds. Now lovage is rarely seen and hard to buy, perhaps because it takes up too much room in the herb garden, or perhaps because its flavour is too strong for modern tastes. I must admit to preferring celery leaves, which can be used as a replacement for lovage, and they give a similar flavour, but in a gentler, subtler way. Lovage is useful as a pot herb. Although only the very young leaves are tender enough to eat, the older ones may be used as part of a bouquet garni or for flavouring stocks when you have no celery to hand.

Cultivation

Lovage is a hardy perennial, easy to grow so long as you give it plenty of room. It does best in a fairly rich soil, in full sun or partial shade. It dies down to ground level each winter, when it may be increased, if desired, by root division. Then it sends out new shoots in the spring.

Medicinal

All parts of lovage possess medicinal qualities, although their use is not advised for pregnant women. An infusion made from the seeds, leaves or roots may be taken for rheumatism, while one made from fresh or dried leaves is good for treating urinary troubles and jaundice. Lovage is also effective as a diuretic, a carminative and a gargle.

recipes using lovage, see pages: 92; 127; 137; 146

lemon balm ~~Melissa officinalis~~

Melissa officinalis

Lemon balm originated in the Mediterranean region. It is a pretty plant with white or yellowish flowers and a very vigorous growth. The aromatic leaves give off a lemon scent when crushed and they were once widely used as a strewing herb. Lemon balm should always be included in a scented garden or a bee garden, for it is very attractive to bees and gives a good flavour to the honey.

In the kitchen its uses are various. The leaves have a slightly scented lemon flavour, like a cross between lemon rind and lemon grass. They may be used as a substitute for either of them, chopped and added to stuffings and salads or used whole in fruit cups. They also make an excellent infusion.

Cultivation

Lemon balm is a perennial plant, growing 45–75 cm (1½ –2½ feet) high. It is best grown on poor soil, and should never be dressed with manure or fertilizer, or the growth will become too vigorous.

Medicinal

Lemon balm is used as a cure for nervous afflictions, insomnia, depression and palpitations. A liqueur, *eau de mélisse*, made by French monks in the seventeenth century was used to cure headaches.

recipe using lemon balm, see page 116

mint

Mint is part of the vast family of herbs called *Labiatae*, which also includes sage, thyme, marjoram, oregano, rosemary, basil, savory and lemon balm, among others. All except basil originated in the Mediterranean and many have been in use since ancient times.

There are some twenty-five varieties of mint, ranging in size from the giant Bowles' mint to the tiny pennyroyal, but their tendency to cross-fertilize has resulted in a wide number of hybrids. From a culinary point of view, only two or three are of interest. Culinary mint is a hybrid of two wild mints: horsemint and spearmint. It may adopt the characteristics of its parents in varying proportions, which is why each mint plant tastes different. Nor will its seed run true to form, so a valued plant must always be propagated by cuttings, rather than seed.

Spearmint, the common or garden mint, is one of the most popular for culinary use. It grows about 60 cm (2 feet) tall, has smooth bright green leaves and bears small white flowers in summer. Bowles' mint, a hybrid of spearmint and apple mint grows up to 1.5 m (5 feet) high, with blue flowers and soft downy leaves. The prettiest mint is apple mint, with variegated white-and-green leaves and a good flavour. Eau-de-Cologne mint, basil mint, pineapple mint and ginger mint are all appealing plants, but too scented for culinary use.

Whereas mint was once used mainly as a digestive, an antidote to rich, fatty food, as in mint sauce with roast lamb, its potential has now been reassessed, and its fresh, cool, juicy character recognized. It blends well with tomatoes or cucumbers, coriander and yogurt in cold soups and salads. In India it is made into a fresh chutney, as a cool contrast to curries.

Cultivation

Mint is a perennial, and all too easy to grow. Since it has a creeping rootstock, it tends to take over the garden unless its roots are contained within a large flower pot or metal bucket. Because of its tendency to cross-hybridize, each variety should be kept apart from other mints.

Mint may be propagated by planting cuttings or small pieces of root 5 cm (2 inches) deep and 5 cm (2 inches) apart, in rows 20–25 cm (8–10 inches) distant. This should be done in late winter or early spring, in moist soil and partial shade.

Medicinal

Spearmint and peppermint are the varieties of mint that are most often used medicinally, primarily as antispasmodics and carminatives, and in conjunction with other remedies for colds.

From left: ginger mint, spearmint, Bowles' apple mint and eau de Cologne mint

recipes using mint, see pages: 144; 165; 171; 180; 192; 195; 199

watercress

Nasturtium officinale

Watercress grows wild, in streams, ditches and water meadows. Although it is easily found, it must be treated with caution, for it can be a dangerous carrier of diseases, including typhoid. Unless the water in which it grows is known to be clean for several kilometres upstream, free from sewage or cattle drinking, it is best avoided. If some doubt lingers, then the watercress should always be cooked, never eaten raw.

The cultivation of watercress began almost 200 years ago and is now done on a huge scale. The commercially grown product has much larger leaves than the wild plant, but the flavour varies widely.

Watercress is an extremely valuable food, just as delicious in its way as more fashionable leaves like rocket, mâche and mizuna. It is also very adaptable and can be used equally well raw or cooked. Its depth of flavour makes it a perfect foil for bland foods and enables it to stand up to generous amounts of cream, in cold soups for instance, without being overwhelmed. It is so full of flavour that it needs no extra seasoning, and is therefore very useful for people on salt-free diets.

Cultivation

Watercress is not easy to grow, since it involves grubbing about in muddy streams and all the frustrations that ensue with underwater planting. If you still want to try, you must first locate a suitable source of clean water. Watercress likes to grow with its roots underwater, in mud, and its tips in the open air. Therefore the water should be no more than 7–10 cm (3–4 inches) deep. The seed may be sown in seedboxes in early summer or autumn, then planted out *in situ* some 15 cm (6 inches) apart. It is probably simpler to divide a plant.

Medicinal

Watercress is rich in iron and other minerals, and in vitamin C. In the sixteenth century it was used as an antiscorbutic. It is also effective in combating bronchial problems and stimulating the circulation.

recipes using watercress, see pages: 168; 181

Ocimum basilicum,
O. minimum

basil

Basil is an annual, a low-growing plant with bright green leaves and small white flowers. It is one of the most tender and fragile of summer herbs, with a unique flavour, both delicate and intense. Basil grew first in India, where it is considered a holy plant and can be found growing around Hindu temples, but being holy, it is not eaten. In Greece the small-leafed bush basil is thought to bring good luck. Like the Indians, the Greeks do not eat basil.

It is probably most appreciated for its culinary virtues in Liguria, in and around Genoa, where pesto was invented. This marvellous sauce for pasta and gnocchi is made with basil, pine nuts and two cheeses – Sardo and Grana – pounded to a fragrant paste with olive oil.

There are many basil varieties. The large lettuce-leafed basil from Naples is handsome and easy to use in the kitchen. The Genoese favour a smaller-leafed variety with an excellent flavour. The very small-leafed bush basil, as seen in Greece, is pretty but less remarkable for cooking, while the beautiful dark opal basil deserves a place in the herb garden on looks alone, although its flavour is less intense than that of the green-leafed varieties.

The essential oil of basil is one of the most volatile and evaporates quickly when subjected to heat, so the herb is best added to dishes after cooking, almost as a garnish, or to cold food. It has a great affinity with tomatoes and with bland cheeses like mozzarella, as in the ubiquitous but delicious tomato and mozzarella salad.

Cultivation

Basil must be sown from seed each year in spring, then planted out in light, rich soil some 20 cm (8 inches) apart. The little plants should be kept well watered until they are firmly rooted. Basil needs the maximum of warmth to bring out its true flavour, so choose a sunny, sheltered spot or grow it under glass until midsummer.

Medicinal

The fresh or dried leaves or flowers may be made into an infusion for treating migraine, nervous tension, constipation and insomnia. An infusion or gargle can be helpful for treating coughs and sore throats.
Basil is a natural disinfectant; a poultice made from the crushed leaves or a cloth soaked in a strong infusion can be used to dress snake bites and the stings of wasps, bees and hornets.

recipes using basil, see pages: 135; 157

marjoram *Origanum majorana*, O.onites

There are two main types of marjoram: sweet marjoram (*Origanum majorana*) and pot marjoram (*O. onites*). *O. vulgare* (opposite) is a third, closely related variety. Both come from the Mediterranean region: sweet marjoram from North Africa, pot marjoram from southern Europe. In their native habitat they are grown as perennials, but in harsher climates they are best treated as annuals, for they rarely survive the winter. Pot marjoram is the more robust and may be grown as a perennial in milder climates.

Sweet marjoram, which is also known as knotted marjoram, grows about 60 cm (2 feet) high, with small, pale green leaves and light mauve and white flowers. This is the variety most often used for cooking, for it has a delicate, warm, sweet flavour. Pot marjoram is stronger, indeed almost too strong, and is best kept for robust dishes. All varieties of marjoram go well with tomatoes, pasta, chicken, veal and most vegetable dishes. Pot marjoram may be added to dishes during the cooking, but the more delicate sweet marjoram is best added when the cooking is virtually finished.

Cultivation

Sweet marjoram may be grown from seed sown in early spring. The seed is sometimes mixed with sand, then sown in drills 23 cm (9 inches) apart or simply scattered in a warm sunny spot in light rich soil. Do not expect sweet marjoram to survive the winter unless it is grown in pots and brought indoors.

Pot marjoram may be propagated by root cuttings or root division in spring or early autumn, then planted outside 30 cm (12 inches) apart.

Both varieties dry remarkably well, and some whole plants should be cut during flowering and dried for winter use.

Medicinal

Sweet marjoram is a carminative and an excellent digestive aid, but pot marjoram has no known medicinal uses.

recipes using marjoram, see pages: 96; 127

oregano

This is wild marjoram, familiar to many people as the *rigani* of Greece. Closely related to marjoram (*O. majorana*), it originated in southern Europe. Although a perennial in origin, oregano is best grown as an annual in northern climates. It is stronger and spicier than marjoram, and is the herb used by Italians in pizzas and pizza-style tomato sauces. Oregano is a robust herb with an unusually stable essential oil; this means that it can be dried very successfully and withstands fairly long periods of heat, so may be added to dishes early in the cooking process.

Cultivation

Oregano is propagated by root cuttings or root division in the spring or early autumn. Plant out the little plants about 30 cm (12 inches foot) apart. Oregano is a tender plant and will not survive a cold winter out of doors.

Medicinal

Oregano is the most powerful of the marjoram tribe for medicinal purposes, and it has long been recognized for its properties as a sedative and calming agent, and as a diuretic, tonic and gargle.

recipes using oregano, see pages: 127; 145; 146

35

parsley

Petroselinum crispum, P. crispum neapolitanum

Parsley, a native of southern Europe, has been growing wild for at least 400 years. The earliest form of cultivated parsley had flat leaves, but the curly-leafed form, *Petroselinum crispum*, later became more popular in Britain and the United States. Flat-leaf parsley (*P. crispum neapolitanum*), has always been preferred in continental Europe.

For the past fifty-odd years, parsley has been grievously misused in most cuisines. Often used merely as a garnish, its many strengths have been ignored. Now, thanks to a growing interest in healthy eating and an enthusiasm for Middle Eastern dishes, it is coming back in force. I prefer flat-leaf parsley, both for flavour and texture, and use it almost always, except in a few traditional English dishes where the curly-leafed variety seems more appropriate.

Parsley mixes well with other herbs, as in the classic bouquet garni and *fines herbes*. It is also good with basil, and with mint, as in the Lebanese salad called *fattoush*. It goes splendidly with bland foods, like noodles and grain, and makes a great sandwich, thickly layered between slices of buttered wholegrain bread.

It is unwise to pick wild parsley for use in the kitchen, as it is hard to distinguish from the poisonous hemlock.

Above: from left, curly parsley and flat-leaf parsley

Cultivation

Parsley is a biennial, but is best treated as an annual and dug after its first year, for during the second year it concentrates on producing stalks and flowers, while the leaves are almost nonexistent and unsatisfactory in flavour. It is easily grown, but may take as long as six weeks to germinate. It should be sown 3 mm (⅛ inch) deep, in drills some 25 cm (10 inches) apart, and later thinned out to 15 cm (6 inches). Alternatively, the seed may be scattered over the ground, with a layer of finely sieved compost sprinkled over it.

Medicinal

Rich in vitamins A, B and C, parsley is also a storehouse of iron and calcium. It is a natural antiseptic, a diuretic, and an effective treatment for hepatitis, rheumatic disorders and gout.

recipes using parsley, see pages: 118; 127; 128; 135; 137; 145; 149; 153; 192

purslane

There are many varieties of purslane, but the most common one is *Portulaca oleracea*, the green purslane which is sometimes called 'continental watercress'. It is quite unusual, and easy to recognize once you know it, with round fleshy stalks bearing a rosette of leaves at the top. It grew first in India, but was being widely grown – and flourishing as a weed – in Elizabethan England. Purslane is a popular salad plant in Greece, Turkey and the Middle East. It is a vital part of the Lebanese salad called *fattoush*, in which it is used in conjunction with large quantities of flat-leaf parsley and mint. Although they can be cooked, the young leaves are most often used raw in salads, while the older stalks are used for making pickles.

Winter purslane (*Claytonia perfoliata*) bears little resemblance to green purslane. It is a low-growing plant, very pretty, with small trumpet-shaped leaves. Grown in an unheated greenhouse, or in a plastic tunnel, it makes a good leaf for winter salads.

Cultivation

Green purslane is an annual, best sown in spring in drills 30 cm (12 inches) apart. The seedlings should later be thinned to 23 cm (9 inches) apart. They thrive in a sunny open position, in well-drained soil. Like the other purslanes, winter purslane is also an annual, and easy to grow from seed.

Medicinal

Purslane is a valuable medicament and may be used in a number of ways. The juice may be drunk freshly pressed, to treat coughs, or used to soak dressings for applying to sores, inflamed areas and painful gums. Whole leaves, fresh and lightly crushed, can be used as a poultice to treat headaches, eye strain and gout.

salad burnet
Poterium
sanguisorba

Salad burnet is a perennial which grows wild all over France. It is a pretty plant, like a round cushion of leaf stems bearing small toothed leaves. The red and green flowers are borne in midsummer on tall stalks. A variety of burnet was grown in Britain in Tudor times and was later taken to America by the early settlers.

The young leaves have a delicious flavour, mild and subtle, redolent of cucumbers. They have one of the least robust of flavours, however, and it is best to use them raw, scattered over salads or chilled soups, in cucumber sandwiches or over scrambled eggs. Salad burnet also is an excellent herb for flavouring vinegar for use in salad dressings.

Cultivation

Salad burnet must be grown from seed, and this should be done every year, for the young leaves of new plants are the most tender. Sow the seed in spring, in well-drained garden soil, and thin out later to 30 cm (12 inches) apart. While the flower heads should really be picked off as they form to encourage leaf growth, if some are left, they will self-seed naturally.

Medicinal

Salad burnet is a nutritious plant, rich in vitamin C. The leaves may be used, fresh or dried, to make infusions for the prevention of infectious diseases. They are effective against gout and rheumatism, and encourage perspiration in cases of fever. Infusions also act as an aid to digestion, a tonic and a mild diuretic. Fresh leaves may be used whole as a poultice to promote the healing of wounds.

recipe using salad burnet, see page 192

rose

Roses were widely grown in herb gardens in England in Elizabethan and Stuart times. As well as their obvious use in pot pourri, roses were used to make rose water, rose-flavoured honey and syrups for flavouring ices and other sweet dishes. Rose petals and buds were gathered and crystallized for decorating cakes, and used fresh in sandwiches.

The most popular roses for use in the kitchen and sitting room are still the old varieties, in particular the damask rose (*Rosa damascena*) and the apothecary's rose (*R. gallica officinalis*), which have never been improved upon for depth of flavour or scent. In Turkey roses have been an important part of the cuisine for centuries. The sweet tooth for which the Turks are famous, combined with their love of perfumed flavours, accounts for the high esteem in which such things as rose water and rose syrup are held. A delicious scented syrup called *shrub* is made with roses, using both flowers and leaves.

Rose water is also very popular in the countries of the Mahgreb, on the southern shores of the Mediterranean. In Tunisia, Algeria and Morocco it is used to flavour sweet pastry dishes filled with pistachios. The dried buds of a variety of damask rose, called *coeurs de rose*, are widely used in Morocco in complex spice blends, like the famous *ras al-hanout*, which combines more than thirty different spices and is mixed to order, and to your individual taste, in the spice shops.

Medicinal

Roses have many therapeutic properties. As a small child growing up during World War II, I remember picking rose hips in the hedgerows to make rose-hip syrup, a valuable source of vitamin C. According to the famed herbalist Maurice Mességué, an infusion of roses has valuable properties that help in curing inflammation of the bronchial tubes and of the digestive passages. The same infusion can be used with effect to counteract the destructive effect of antibiotics on the internal bacteria.

recipe using rose, see page 198

rosemary *Rosmarinus officinalis*

This attractive herb grew first in the eastern Mediterranean. In its chosen surroundings it is an evergreen perennial, but in northern climes it often fails to survive the winter. It is a pretty plant, a bushy shrub with spiky leaves like needles, dark green on top and silvery-grey underneath. In early summer the branches are decked with pale blue flowers, which attract the bees.

Rosemary is much used as a seasoning in France, particularly in Provence, and in Italy. It has a powerful flavour, and should be used with caution if its camphor overtones are not to become too dominant. It is best used alone, although it is mixed with thyme and other Mediterranean herbs in the mixture of dried herbs called *herbes de Provence* (see page 49). Two or three sprigs of rosemary are often laid around a leg of lamb or a chicken while it is roasting. It also goes wonderfully well with roast, grilled or fried potatoes.

Rosemary is one of the few herbs that dries well, preserving all its flavour, although, as it is an evergreen, the leaves can equally well be left on the shrub and picked as needed throughout the year. If picking them for drying, the best time is in autumn, when the plant produces marvellous shoots 20–23 cm (8–9 inches) long. Don't ever cut it back to the old wood – always leave the last whorl of leaves on the new shoots intact. Rosemary was intended to be nibbled by goats, who would never eat beyond the tender tips.

Cultivation

Growing rosemary from seed is a lengthy business; better to buy a plant or get cuttings from a friend. These should be about 15 cm (6 inches) long. Plant in sand, then transplant the following spring. Root division may also be carried out in autumn or early spring.

Rosemary grows slowly, but needs plenty of space, for it can grow up to 18 m (6 feet) high. It needs some protection from frost, so it is best grown in a sunny, sheltered spot, or in a large pot, which can be brought indoors in winter.

Medicinal

Rosemary is valued for its medicinal properties as a diuretic, a stimulant and a gargle.

sorrel

Various forms of sorrel grow wild in Europe, while still others are found throughout the United States. The British and American cultivated form derives from *Rumex acetosa*, while the French one comes from *R. scutatus*. The latter is superior in terms of flavour, being more acidic, and these plants should be acquired whenever possible.

Sorrel was popular in Britain in medieval times, but was later more or less forgotten, while in France it retained its popularity. It is one of those oddly placed plants halfway between a leaf vegetable and a herb. It has merit in both roles. When cooked as a vegetable, it resembles spinach, but with an added tang that gives a lift to soups and sauces alike. Its water content is very high, so it shrinks dramatically on cooking. Its other disadvantage is that it loses its colour on cooking, turning a dull brown, while its texture becomes slimy. When combined with spinach in purées, sauces and soups, this is not apparent. When treated as a herb, its value is as a garnish, used raw, when its tart acidic quality adds enormously to bland, creamy dishes.

Cultivation

Sorrel is a perennial, growing in a sturdy clump some 45–60 cm (18–24 inches) high. It is easily grown from seed, and successive sowings are advised, since only the young leaves should be used. Seed should be sown in spring or autumn, in drills 35 cm (14 inches) apart. Alternatively, sorrel may be propagated by root division in spring.

Medicinal

Sorrel is rich in potassium and in vitamins A, B and C. Alas, it has a high oxalic acid content and should therefore be avoided by people with gout, rheumatism or arthritis. The roots and seeds are efficacious infused and drunk as a treatment for urinary troubles, colic, dysentery, diarrhoea and stomach aches. An infusion of fresh or dried leaves may be used as a diuretic, antiscorbutic, tonic or mild laxative.

recipe using sorrel, see page 162

sage Salvia officinalis

Sage originated on the northern shores of the Mediterranean. It is a perennial, a low-growing shrub about 30–45 cm (12–18 inches) high, with soft, velvety leaves of pale grey-green. Its flowers are pink or mauve. All the varieties of sage are pretty plants, some – like the purple, red, golden or variegated sage – especially so. But the common or garden sage is best for use in the kitchen. Unlike most herbs, sage can withstand long cooking without loss of flavour, for its essential oil is a stable one. For the same reason it dries well.

I have only recently become converted to sage, having been put off for years by the musty taste of dried sage used to excess in sausages. Now, however, I have learnt to love it, and use it constantly. Whole leaves can be fried crisp and scattered over pasta, gnocchi or grilled vegetables. They can also be coated in a light batter and deep-fried, then served as a tempting first course, with a salad, or as a garnish for plain grilled chicken or gammon. Freshly picked leaves may be chopped and stirred into an onion purée or apple sauce for serving with goose, duck, pork or sausages. Indeed sage has a particular affinity for onions and with them makes a classic stuffing for poultry or pork. Along with finely chopped spring onions or chives it is also a delicious flavouring ingredient for savoury breads or plain pancake batter to be cooked for a savoury filling. Sage is a powerful herb, rather like rosemary, and must be treated with caution. Again like rosemary, it is best used alone, for its slightly camphorous flavour does not mix well with other herbs.

Above: from left, sage
purple, sage golden, sage
tricolour, sage green

Cultivation

Sage is easy to grow, given a sheltered spot in partial shade, but it may need some protection from frost, as it is only semi-hardy. It is not hard to grow from seed, but it will not be ready to pick until its second year. The seed may be sown in early spring under glass, then transplanted into the open a couple of months later.

It is quicker to grow sage from cuttings taken in late spring and planted out of doors, some 40–45 cm (16–18 inches) apart.

Medicinal

Sage has has been used by physicians for centuries. It is a natural antiseptic, a tonic and stimulant. It is also an antispasmodic and an antidote to fatigue. It aids the digestion of rich and fatty foods. Fresh sage leaves make an excellent herb tea, which acts as an effective digestive.

summer and winter savory

Savory is a pretty plant, growing 15–45 cm (6–18 inches) high, with narrow tapering leaves and small pink flowers. There are two varieties: summer or garden savory *Satureja hortensis*, which is an annual, and winter or mountain savory *S. montana*, which is biennial. Summer savory is a native of the Mediterranean, while winter savory grew first in the mountainous regions of southern Europe and North Africa. Both varieties were brought to Britain and northern Europe by the Romans, and were taken to America by the early colonists.

Well known in Elizabethan England, when bitter herbs were favoured, savory is rarely seen in Britain now, although both varieties are popular in France. There they are used as a flavouring for bean dishes, especially broad beans, and in Provence a wild savory called *poivre d'ane* is used to coat a ewes'-milk cheese called *banon*.

I have an aversion to winter savory, which is a truly bitter herb and cannot be eaten raw. But summer savory is milder, with much to be said for it. Its very specific use is as a flavour enhancer, to strengthen the effect of other herbs, or alone to enhance the flavour of the food itself. Even a jar of commercially made tomato and basil sauce warmed through slowly with ½ teaspoon of dried savory will take on a new character, as the herb mellows it. Both summer and winter savoury are very potent and should be used in carefully judged amounts.

Cultivation

Savory likes a rich soil. It can be grown from seed sown in spring, preferably *in situ*, for it does not like being moved. (Both varieties can be grown from seed, but in my opinion only summer savory is worth the trouble.) Thin out plants to 20 cm (8 inches). Pick most of the plants to ground level just before they flower and dry them. Savory dries exceptionally well. Plants left to flower will seed themselves.

Medicinal

Savory is best used as an infusion, which can be made with fresh or dried leaves and flowers. This is primarily a digestive. It is also a diuretic, and beneficial to people suffering from gout, rheumatism or breathing disorders.

Above: from top, winter savory and summer savory.

mustard
Sinapis alba, Brassica nigra, B. juncea

There are many different varieties of mustard and two of these – white (*Sinapis alba*) and brown (*Brassica juncea*) – are grown primarily for their seeds, which are used in making mustard powder. Black mustard (*Brassica nigra*) is no longer grown commercially, having been superseded by brown varieties. Black and white mustard grew first around the Mediterranean, while brown mustard comes from the Himalayas.

Until recently the main use of white mustard seedlings was in sandwiches, mixed with cress. Only the first pair of leaves, or cotyledons, are used for this purpose, although the plants can, of course, be left in the ground to produce larger leaves for use in salads.

Now, however, in their never-ending search for new salad leaves to please their customers, chefs and their suppliers are experimenting with a range of mustards imported from the East. These are the mustard greens and red and black mustards, which are widely used in South-east Asia, India, China and Japan. These peppery little leaves are delicious when used like rocket or mizuna in salads of mixed leaves. Alternatively, they may be allowed to grow a stage larger, when they can be braised or stir-fried. The danger with all the mustards is that once they are past the seedling stage, the leaves have a tendency to become hairy.

Cultivation

All the mustards are easily grown, although it may be hard to find seeds of black or brown mustard or mustard greens. Mustard will grow in virtually any soil and, although it prefers humidity and warmth, it is remarkably tolerant of frost. It can be grown from spring onwards and picked at any time.

Medicinal

Only the seeds are ever used in this context, usually in a poultice, bath or infusion. The poultice is made with the crushed seeds stuck on sheets of brown paper. It is very effective for treating muscular pains (such as lumbago, neuralgia, rheumatism and arthritis), chilblains, pneumonia, bronchitis and congestion of the chest and lungs. Foot and hand baths containing mustard seeds are given, while whole baths are are usually thought to be too powerful for most people.

comfrey

Symphitum officinale

Comfrey is a perennial, growing some 60–75 cm (2–3 feet) high, with large, hairy leaves and spikes of purple, mauve or white flowers which are borne all through the summer. It grew first in western Europe, spreading across from Britain and Spain to the Asian border.

  Although rarely seen nowadays, comfrey was once a popular plant in medieval herb gardens, valued as much for its medicinal qualities as for its culinary use. The young leaves may be cooked like spinach or mixed with other leaves in a green salad. They may also be made into fritters by dipping in a light batter and frying in deep oil.

Cultivation

Comfrey is easily grown from seed sown in early spring, then thinned to 30 cm (12 inches). It will seed itself and can also be propagated by root division in the spring. It needs plenty of space, for the roots tend to spread, and it also demands copious watering.

Medicinal

Comfrey, especially the wild variety, is an important natural medicament. It has the power to soothe, whether it be stomach troubles, like ulcers, dysentery and diarrhoea, or inflammation of any sort. Fresh or dried leaves, or the root may be made into infusions for treating these conditions.

recipe using comfrey, see page 155

45

dandelion *Taraxacum officinale*

The dandelion is a native of Europe, a wild meadow plant with deeply indented leaves and bright yellow flowers, which become transformed into balls of downy fluff. It is one of the most valuable wild plants, both as food and for its medicinal properties. The young leaves may be eaten raw in salads, and form part of the Provençal salad called *mesclun*, consisting of mixed tiny bitter leaves tossed with garlic-flavoured croûtons. The older leaves can be cooked like spinach and served warm with olive oil and lemon juice. In the past the root was often dried, roasted and ground for use as a substitute for coffee.

Leaves to be eaten raw should be gathered in spring before the flowers have formed, for after that point they become too bitter to be palatable. This can be offset by blanching: simply invert a large flowerpot over the plant for seven to ten days before picking, with a piece of slate over the hole so that the dandelion grows in total darkness. This renders the leaves pale and reduces the bitterness.

The cultivated form of dandelion is infinitely superior from the culinary point of view, although not the medicinal one. The leaves are larger, with a far milder flavour, and they do not need to be blanched. These are ideal for making that excellent dish of wilted dandelion salad with diced bacon, dressed with the warm bacon fat and white wine vinegar.

Cultivation

Dandelions are all too easy to grow from seed. The main problem is to stop them seeding themselves everywhere in the garden. With this in mind, be sure to pick off all the flower heads before the seeds start to form and fly.

Medicinal

The flowers and the large tough leaves of dandelions may be used to make tea, while the roots can be infused in white wine for three days to make a powerful tonic. Both the wine and the tea may be taken – without much pleasure, it must be said – as an effective diuretic, digestive or liver stimulant.

thyme

There are about 100 different varieties, but the one most used in the kitchen is the common or garden thyme, *Thymus vulgaris*. The thymes grow 7–30 cm (3–12 inches) high, with tiny oval grey-green leaves and tiny flowers in shades of pink, mauve, red and white.

Thyme is one of the most useful culinary herbs. Its essential oil is remarkably robust, so it can withstand long cooking and is equally effective used fresh, semi-dried or dried. There is rarely much point in drying it since you can pick it all through the year, except for the two months when it is flowering and the leaves lose their flavour. If picking thyme in bulk for drying, you can cut it twice: once just before flowering, then remove the flower heads and allow the plant to grow again before making your second cut.

Thyme marries well with other herbs, as in the classic bouquet garni (see page 49), where it is combined with parsley and bay, and in *herbes de Provence* (see page 49). It goes well with most Provençal dishes and can be substituted for marjoram or oregano in many others.

Wild thyme, *T. serpyllum*, grows in the United States and most of northern Europe, including Britain. It is a low-growing variety, generally considered inferior in flavour to the common thyme, except in France, where it is called *serpolet*. It is very popular in Lebanon, where it is called *zaatar* and is mixed in equal parts with toasted sesame seeds to coat small soft cheeses called *labneh*, which are eaten for breakfast. Lemon thyme, *T. citriodorus*, is a useful herb for cooking, having the usual thyme flavour overlaid with lemon.

Cultivation

Thyme may be grown from seed sown *in situ* in spring, then later thinned out to 30 cm (12 inches) apart. If growing more than one variety, keep them separate as they hybridize easily. Thyme may also be raised from cuttings taken in early summer. The creeping forms can be increased by division in late summer. These low-growing varieties are the most hardy; the others need some protection from frost. Alternatively, they may be grown in large pots and moved indoors during the worst of the winter.

Medicinal

Thyme was highly valued by the Romans, who used it as a cure for melancholy and an aid to failing memory. It is also an antiseptic because of its high thymol content, a diuretic, digestive and antispasmodic.

Above: from left, English winter thyme, broad-leaf thyme and lemon thyme.

recipes using thyme, see pages: 96; 128; 146

nasturtium *Tropaeolum majus, T. minus*

The nasturtium grew first in the Peruvian forests, and is believed to have been brought to Europe by the Spaniards in the sixteenth century. A decorative plant, the nasturtium has long been included in herb gardens, and with good reason, for every part of it is edible and rich in minerals and vitamins. The common nasturtium (*T. majus*) is a climbing plant and may grow as much as 3 m (10 feet) high if given adequate support. Alternatively, it may be left to sprawl along the ground. There is also a dwarf form (*T minus*), which flowers even more profusely and is probably more suitable for small gardens.

The nasturtium has pretty, light green leaves, which are blunt-edged and almost round in shape. The trumpet-shaped flowers are orange, red or yellow, with small purple blotches. The leaves have a warm peppery flavour, not unlike watercress. (The Latin name of watercress is *Nasturtium officinale*, which is often confusing.) The flowers have a similar, milder flavour and look very effective scattered over a green salad. Both seeds and flower buds may be pickled in vinegar and used in the same way as capers.

Cultivation

Nasturtiums are annuals, easily grown from seed sown *in situ* in spring. They grow quickly and will flower two to three months after sowing. They prefer a moist soil free from lime, but it should not be too rich, for this will encourage leafy growth at the expense of flowers. Be careful not to overpick the leaves; at least one-third should be left on the plant if it is to thrive. The flowers should be picked as soon as they have opened, or even before, while the seeds are ready once they have filled out.

Medicinal

In the past nasturtiums were used to combat scurvy, for they are rich in sulphur. They also contain valuable amounts of iron and vitamin C, and have been used for centuries as a tonic, stimulant and aphrodisiac.

herb mixtures

bouquet garni

This is the customary combination of herbs for flavouring liquid dishes, such as soups and stews, in the French classical tradition. Usually consisting of 1 bay leaf, 1 thyme sprig and 3 parsley stalks, it is often enclosed by a piece of celery stalk or a piece of leek and tied together with string. Alternatively, it is sometimes wrapped in a small square of muslin, tied with thin string.

fines herbes

A subtle and carefully balanced mixture of delicate summer herbs, this combination cannot be improved upon for flavouring omelettes and other egg dishes, salads of soft, mild lettuce leaves, and cream sauces. The classic combination usually consists of equal parts of chervil, chives, parsley and tarragon.

herbes de Provence

Unlike the *fines herbes* combination described above, this is a mixture of dried Provençal herbs, which contributes its own inimitable flavour to dishes of that region. Always included are the two main ingredients, rosemary and thyme, while the others usually consist of marjoram and basil, and sometimes also savory and/or tarragon.

Below: bouquet garni

recipe using herbes de Provence, see page 96

spice directory
50–89

dill seeds
Anethum graveolens

Dill is grown primarily for its leaves, which are used fresh, as a herb, but in Russia, Scandinavia and the United States the seeds are also prized. In Russia they are used mainly for pickling fish and vegetables, while in the Scandinavian countries they are added to potato dishes and used in baking rye bread. The dill pickles, so popular with pastrami and salt beef sandwiches in America, are made with small cucumbers pickled in vinegar flavoured with dill seeds. In America the two forms of dill are differentiated by calling them dill weed (the leaf) and dill seed.

Dill is an annual, a native of the Mediterranean region and southern parts of Russia. It is very similar to fennel in appearance, but milder and more delicate in flavour. (Fennel and dill should not be grown in close proximity, for they will cross-pollinate and their flavours merge.) The yellow flowers are borne in umbels in midsummer and the seeds should be left to ripen on the plant before harvesting and drying. They may then be used in the kitchen or be kept to sow the following spring.

celery seeds

Celery seeds are not easy to find in the supermarkets, so it is well worth growing your own. Now that a self-blanching variety of celery has been developed, cultivation is far easier. Celery is a biennial, and produces seed only in its second year. During the first year the stems and leaves may be used. Celery seeds are a useful flavouring for soups and stews instead of fresh celery. Celery salt is the best seasoning for hard-boiled eggs, and the essential accompaniment to gulls' eggs during their short season. To make celery salt, pound 4 parts celery seed with 1 part sea salt in a mortar. For cultivation and medicinal use, see celery leaves, page 16.

paprika

Paprika is made from mild varieties of capsicum, or sweet pepper, which have had their seeds and inner membranes removed before being dried and ground. The capsicum grew wild in Mexico, where it was discovered and was then taken to Europe by the Spaniards in the first part of the sixteenth century.

Paprika was first made in Hungary, after the capsicum had been brought there by the Turks, and became highly popular. It is still a vital flavouring in many Hungarian dishes, particularly goulash. Spanish paprika, called *pimentón*, is slightly different from the Central European variety, being made from a different species of capsicum. In both Spain and Hungary, paprika is manufactured in several grades, based on quality, strength – the hottest is almost comparable to chilli powder – and price.

Paprika should be bought in small amounts and used quickly, for, even more than with other spices, both flavour and colour deteriorate quickly. The best quality paprika is a bright red, which is one of its virtues; a dusty, blood-red paprika is probably stale.

cayenne
Capsicum frutescens

Cayenne, or red pepper, is not related to black or white pepper, which is the fruit of a climbing vine. It is made from the dried and ground flesh and seeds of the fiercely hot bird, or bird's eye, chilli, which belongs to the same family as the mild red and green pepper, the capsicum.

Cayenne reached Britain from India in 1548, at a time when highly spiced food was at the peak of its appeal. Yet over 400 years later, cayenne has retained its popularity in the West, adding heat to spicy dishes, curries and pastes, and lightly pepping up the flavour of savouries, like Welsh rarebit and cheese straws.

recipes using cayenne, see pages: 97; 101; 168

chillies
Capsicum frutescens

Chillies, tiny red berries with a fiery heat, grew first in the Amazon region of South America and in Mexico. Even before the arrival of Christopher Columbus, chillies had spread northward to the south-west of North America, and eastward to the Caribbean. Columbus took them with him when he returned to Spain, and from there they reached Portugal. The Portuguese carried chillies with them to India when establishing their trading posts at Cochin. The arrival of the chilli revolutionized Indian cooking. Until then, the only sources of 'heat' had been the peppercorn and the mustard seed.

The capsaicin, which is the heat-producing element, is contained in the inner membrane, the veins and the seeds. Thus the heat content may be decreased by discarding the membrane and all, or at least some, of the seeds. In the case of dried chillies, the inner membrane has more or less vanished, and the seeds are easily shaken out and discarded.

On the whole, the hottest chillies are the tiny ones, like the tabasco, cayenne and bird or bird's eye. I tend to settle for the middle range, 5–7/10 on the heat-scale, as the very hot habañero deadens my whole mouth, tongue and throat. My current favourite is the chipotle, a smoke-dried jalapeño, 6–7/10, with a delicious, subtle, smoky flavour.

To relieve the burning sensation after eating too hot a chilli, the best remedy is cold dairy food – ice cream, yogurt, milk – or bananas. After handling chillies, do not touch your eyes, lips or sensitive skin until you have washed your hands in warm, soapy water.

Chillies have an amazing effect on the whole system, and can clear the nasal passages and banish colds, apathy and mild depression. They are a forceful stimulant and, by electrifying the saliva glands and digestive juices, they aid the digestive process, especially of starches.

Crushed Chilli Flakes

These are a marvellous short cut for the busy cook who needs to spark up a bland dish. They are quite simply medium hot, dried chilli peppers broken into small pieces. The little red specks of chilli also add visual interest.

Chilli Powder

Chilli powder varies depending on type and country of origin. Indian chilli powder, which provides the hot element in curry powder, is very similar to cayenne powder. They are both made from the dried and ground flesh and seeds of red chillies.

recipes using chillies, see pages: 97; 98; 110; 112; 122; 124; 132; 144; 149; 168; 183; 185; 186; 187; 188; 189; 190; 196; 205

caraway seeds

Caraway is a native of northern Europe and Asia, growing wild in the Himalayas and Siberia. It was prized by the Arabs in ancient times, and was believed to have many magical and medicinal properties. It is a member of the same umbelliferous family as fennel and dill, and is very similar to them in appearance. It is a biennial growing about 60 cm (2 feet) high, with hollow, woody stems and narrow leaves. The seeds are almost identical to those of cumin: small, oval, ribbed and grey-brown. Caraway is often confused with cumin, especially in France, where it is called *cumin des près*.

Caraway seeds are a favourite flavouring in central and northern Europe, especially in Germany, Austria, Finland and the Scandinavian countries, and are also widely used in Jewish cookery. The German word for caraway is *kümmel*, which is also the name of the liqueur that is made from it. Caraway seeds are used to flavour dishes of sauerkraut, potatoes, pork and sausages, and they are added to rye bread. In Alsace a dish of roasted caraway seeds is served with the local Münster cheese. In Britain caraway seeds have lost the popularity they enjoyed in Elizabethan times. Then, they were baked in breads and cakes, and made into small sugar-coated sweets called comfits. According to Elizabeth David in her book *English Bread and Yeast Cookery* (Allen Lane, 1977), these comfits were baked in bread rolls and cakes to give a crunchy effect. They were used in this way in Bath buns, both in the dough itself and scattered over the top after baking. Now caraway seeds are usually used in British cooking only in seed cake, itself a rarely seen relic of the past.

recipes using caraway seeds, see pages: 166; 186; 189

cassia Cinnamomum cassia

Cassia is a native of China, and is now grown widely throughout South-east Asia. It is one of the ingredients of Chinese Five Spice Powder and is the Chinese equivalent of cinnamon, to which it is closely related, but is somewhat stronger and coarser in flavour. Like cinnamon, it is sold in two forms: quills of rolled aromatic bark and ground into powder. The quills are thicker and less tightly rolled (or even flat) than those of cinnamon, and are harder. They are difficult to grind at home, so cassia is best bought ground. Its use should be relegated to savoury dishes such as meat, with the more delicate cinnamon reserved for sweet dishes (although in Germany, Italy and the United States cassia is used in making chocolate). It also works as a digestive when taken in the form of an infusion.

cinnamon

Cinnamon is the thinly rolled inner bark of an evergreen tree that grows mainly in southern India and Sri Lanka, Madagascar and the West Indies. It is used as a flavouring for sweet and savoury dishes. Cinnamon acts as a digestive and stimulant, and calms the stomach. It is also a natural antiseptic.

It has been known in Britain for hundreds of years, but nowadays its use is confined to sweet dishes, like hot cross buns, fruit cakes and mincemeat, and to mulled wine. A mixture of ground cinnamon, nutmeg and cloves is often used to spice bread and cakes. Yet in medieval times, when spices were in more general use in Britain, cinnamon was frequently added to meat or even fish dishes.

In the United States cinnamon is widely used in cakes and pastries, often combined with apples, while cinnamon toast, hot toast spread with sweetened butter flavoured with cinnamon, is a popular snack. Cinnamon is probably most widely used as a flavouring in Turkey and Egypt. In India cinnamon is commonly used in meat and rice dishes, and it features in mild spice mixtures, particularly *garam masala*. It is also one of the ingredients of commercially manufactured curry powder.

recipe using cinnamon, see page 197

Coriandrum
coriander
sativum

Coriander is believed to have been introduced to northern Europe by the Romans, but it is not known whether it was valued for the sake of the berries or the leaves. The berries are the spice and they have a warm 'fruity' flavour. The leaves are the herb. Coriander is used extensively, both as a spice and as a herb, in India and South-east Asia. In Thailand the roots are used more than the leaves or berries.

Coriander is easily grown, so long as the soil is light, friable and gets plenty of sun. Sew the seed in spring in rows 1 cm (½ inch) deep and 20 cm (8 inches) apart. The berries ripen in late summer, when the plant should be cut and left to dry. Then the heads are collected and the berries harvested. Coriander seeds itself readily if allowed to do so. For more information about cultivation and medicinal use, see page 22.

A magical spice that seems to enhance other foods, coriander is equally good used alone and in conjunction with other spices. It is delicious mixed in equal parts with cumin or in more complex blends such as curry powder and *garam masala*. It is an important part of English pickling spice and dishes cooked *à la grecque*. It is good with fish, meat, eggs, vegetables and grains, and in sweet dishes, like spiced cakes and puddings.

Coriander is immensely popular in Tunisia, where it is combined with garlic, caraway seeds and dried chillies in a spice mixture called *Tabil*. It is also frequently used with ground cinnamon and dried rosebuds.

recipes using mustard, see pages: 138; 141; 144; 188; 189

saffron

Saffron is made from the dried stigmas of a species of crocus. This bulb grows 15 cm
(6 inches) high and has a purple flower in the autumn. It must not be confused with the
autumn crocus, *Colchicum autumnale*, which also bears purple flowers in the autumn but
does not produce leaves until the following spring; the stamens of this crocus are poisonous.
Each flower of the *Crocus sativus* has only three pistils, which must first be picked by hand
and then the saffron is extracted, also by hand. Over 4,000 blooms are required to yield
25 g (1 oz) of saffron.

Saffron has always been the most costly of all the spices and in many countries the most
highly prized, but this is a very potent spice and ¼–½ teaspoon is the most that any dish
should need unless it is being made on a large scale.

Saffron is marketed in two forms: whole threads and ground into a powder. It is usually
advisable to buy threads rather than powder, as the latter is easily adulterated, especially in
markets in Third World countries, where marigold or safflower stamens, or even turmeric,
are often added to, or substituted for, the real thing.

A good way to maximize the flavour and colour of threads is by first gently toasting them
in a metal spoon over a low heat, then pounding them in a mortar, adding a couple of
spoonfuls of hot liquid — stock, water or milk — and leaving them to infuse for 5 minutes.
The highly coloured and aromatic liquid can now be added to a dish, preferably towards the
end of its cooking. Powdered saffron can be added instantly to any dish, and is useful in a
dry dish when liquid is not used. But saffron threads can easily be crumbled between the
fingers for this purpose too, so do not despair if that is all you have.

recipes using saffron, see pages: 96; 101; 118; 136; 138; 146; 150; 159; 187

cumin

Cuminum cyminum

Cumin shares certain characteristics with coriander: both originated in the eastern Mediterranean; in both cases it is the fruit, rather than the seed, of the plant that is used as a spice; and both plants are members of the parsley family, *Umbelliferae*. Cumin has narrow, ribbon-like leaves and umbels of small pink or white flowers. The so-called seeds are oblong in shape; greyish in colour. Dry-roasting cumin before grinding, or using whole seeds, brings out the flavour.

One of the most subtle and delicate of all the Indian 'curry' spices, cumin blends remarkably well with coriander and it is used in spice mixtures, such as curry powder and *garam masala*. In India both whole and ground cumin are widely used, and black cumin is much esteemed.

Cumin goes well with fish, vegetables, grains and pulses. Its taste is quite pervasive, so use in moderation. It complements cheese superbly, and wild cumin is used in making Münster cheese in Alsace.

Cumin also has medicinal properties: it helps to dispel flatulence, acts as an antispasmodic and is effective, when used as a poultice, in relieving aches and pains.

recipe using cumin, see page 150

turmeric

Turmeric is one of the less distinguished spices, but because of its low price and easy availability it is also one of the more familiar ones. We find it frequently in curry powders, mustards and relishes like piccalilli, and as a cheap substitute for saffron. It is often used in marinades, and gives an agreeable yellow colouring, similar to saffron, and an appealing earthy taste to cooked dishes.

The plant is of the same family as ginger, but with broader leaves, and has similar rhizomes, but with bright orange flesh, which turns yellow when dried. In India and South-east Asia fresh turmeric is used like fresh ginger, but is much harder to grate or chop. In the West turmeric is available dried, either whole or ground. Because of its rock-like consistency, it is probably best bought ground, but it should be purchased in small quantities and used quickly, for it soon starts to taste musty.

Turmeric is a natural antiseptic, and is also used as a dye, perhaps most notably in the yellow robes of Buddhist monks. It grows wild in the tropical countries of southern Asia, and varies in brightness according to where it grows.

recipes using turmeric, see pages: 138; 144; 150; 188

cardamom
Elettaria cardamomum

The aromatic essence of cardamom is contained within the seeds: small black objects, crowded together, 10–12 at a time, inside the papery pod. The pistachio-green pods are the best; less good are the larger brown pods or those that have been bleached white. The plant is herbaceous, growing 3.5 metres (12 feet) high. It is related to ginger, and is widely grown in tropical regions of India, Sri Lanka and South America.

Cardamom is one of the prime ingredients in commercially made curry powder and in *garam masala*. In Scandinavia and parts of northern Germany and Russia, cardamom is used to flavour liqueurs, while in the Middle East a few cardamom seeds are added to coffee to give that unmistakable perfumed aroma and taste. In the Arab countries the seeds are often chewed, both as a digestive and to sweeten the breath.

recipe using cardamom, see page 177

cloves

Cloves are the immature, unopened flowerbuds of an evergreen tree that grows near the coast of tropical parts of South-east Asia, east Africa and the West Indies. It grew first on the Spice Islands, or Moluccas, and was taken to many lands in Europe by the Romans. It was, at that time, as highly regarded as black peppercorns, a true luxury. In the eighteenth century the cultivation of cloves spread to Madagascar and Zanzibar. Today they are grown in southern India, Sri Lanka, Java, Sumatra, Brazil and the West Indies.

Cloves can be bought whole, still on the stalk, or ground. Unless you plan to use them immediately, it is better to buy them whole, for ground spices soon lose their freshness and taste musty.

Cloves are widely used in conjunction with other spices – usually black peppercorns, nutmeg and cinnamon – or alone, in savoury and sweet dishes, and in drinks. They are commonly stuck in an onion to flavour bread sauce, used to stud the surface of a ham before baking and stuck in apples before baking. They are also added to mulled wine. In India cloves are used in meat and rice dishes, and are one of the spices in *garam masala*. Use in moderation, for their strong aromatic flavour can become over-assertive.

recipes using cloves, see pages: 189; 197

asafoetida

Ferula asafoetida

Asafoetida is an obscure and fascinating substance, little known in the West today, although it was esteemed by the Romans. It is formed from the sap that flows from the roots of a large umbelliferous plant, very like cow parsley in appearance, which is grown mainly in Iran and India. The roots are cut with a knife in early summer and the milky sap that seeps out turns into a hard resin-like substance. It is sold either in block form or ground into powder. When bought in the piece, it must be crushed in a mortar before use. In either form it should be stored in an airtight container, for it has a powerful and unpleasant smell. This disappears on contact with heat, and a delicate onion-like flavour develops. For this reason it is particularly prized by members of Indian sects who are not permitted to eat onions.

As well as flavour, asafoetida has great digestive powers, and helps to combat flatulence. It is used, always in minute quantities, in dishes of dried beans, fresh vegetables and fish.

fennel seeds

Fennel grows wild in southern Europe and in the British Isles. It is very popular in Italy, both as a vegetable and as a flavouring, and the seeds are used in a salami called *finocchiona*, made in florence. Fennel seeds are widely used in Indian cookery, in dishes of meat, fish and vegetables, and in spice mixtures; whole roasted seeds are also chewed after a meal, as a digestive.

The medicinal properties of fennel are many: an infusion of the seeds can be taken as a stimulant, a digestive and a sedative, and as a treatment for bronchial troubles, or used as an eyewash.

There are three varieties of fennel. The one to grow for seeds is wild fennel (*Foeniculum vulgare*); the others (*F. officinale and F. dulce*) are cultivated for use as a vegetable. Fennel is easily grown, and will self-seed if some of the seeds are left to fall naturally. A perennial, growing to about 1.5 m (5 feet) high, it does well in a sunny spot in well-drained soil. Very like dill, angelica and caraway in its pattern of growth, although quite distinct in flavour, fennel has hollow woody stems, finely divided leaves and umbels of yellow flowers.

The seeds are very similar to dill but slightly larger, longer and light greenish-brown. The seed should be sown in spring and may be harvested from midsummer onwards. If preferred, the plants may be propagated by root division in the spring, so that all the seeds can be used as a spice. Fennel and dill should not be grown too close together or they will cross-fertilize.

liquorice Gycyrrhiza glabra

Liquorice is a hardy, herbaceous perennial, a member of the pea family. It is native to south-western Asia, growing wild through Asia Minor. It is a graceful plant, growing 1–1.3 m (3–4 feet) tall, with light, feathery leaves and pale blue flowers, followed by small reddish-brown pods, rather like small pea pods, each containing 3–4 seeds. The tap root grows 1–1.3 m (3–4 feet) deep, and throws off a series of horizontal rhizomes. Both root and rhizomes are used to make the sweet extract for medicinal and other purposes.

Liquorice was used by the ancient Greeks as a medicament for curing coughs and other chest ailments. It has been used for the same purposes by the Italians ever since Roman times, and is still much used in this way in Spain, southern France, Germany, Austria, Russia, Greece and China.

It has been cultivated in Britain since Elizabethan times, especially in Yorkshire, where its use has been primarily for flavouring confectionery. Until the advent of antibiotics after World War II, it was used to sweeten unpalatable medicines such as cascara. It was also used to darken gingerbread, and to flavour beer, tobacco and snuff.

Liquorice is easily grown in full sun, in a well-drained, rich soil, dug 1–1.3 m (3–4 feet) deep and 2–3 m (6–9 feet) wide. It is increased by root division in autumn or spring, and should be permitted to grow undisturbed for 3–5 years before being harvested, to allow a dense root and rhizome system to grow. In their fresh state the roots and rhizomes are wrinkled and fibrous, brown outside and yellowish within. They can be chewed raw to extract the familiar sweetness, or be coarsely grated and infused to make a tea, which can be helpful in treating coughs and sore throats. For commercial use, the rhizomes and roots of liquorice are ground, boiled and evaporated to make the root extract, which is then marketed in stick form or ground again as a spice.

star anise

This unmistakable spice is shaped like a star and has a strong smell of aniseed mixed with liquorice, like an old-fashioned sweet shop. In the centre of each petal-shaped pod is an oval seed, light brown and shiny. The tree from which it comes is an evergreen related to the magnolia and grows wild in China and Japan.

Star anise is much used in Chinese cookery, especially in and around Canton. It is also used in some areas of Indonesia, and in parts of western India, like Goa, that have traded with China in the past.

The flavour of star anise is similar to ordinary aniseed, but stronger and with a more pronounced liquorice element. It is a major ingredient in Chinese five spice powder and is often added whole to dishes of braised meat and poultry. It may be removed before serving, although in the East whole spices, like cinnamon and star anise, are often left in the dish and simply pushed to the side of the plate by each diner.

recipe using star anise, see page 177

69

juniper berries

Juniperus communis

There are many wild species of juniper, but the one whose berries are used in food is native to the British Isles and grows throughout most of northern Europe. It is a small tree or shrub, an evergreen conifer with prickly leaves and small yellow flowers. The berries take two to three years to ripen, so that both ripe and unripe berries may be found on the same bush. The green, unripe berries turn purplish-blue as they ripen; later, when dried, they blacken. The ripe berries are picked in the autumn and dried, or semi-dried, before used.

Juniper berries are used primarily in making gin. They are also much used, especially in Central Europe, in marinades, terrines, sauerkraut, and with game, pork and ham. In Britain, they feature in traditional recipes for spicing beef. The wood gives off a fragrant smoke when burnt, thus scenting a room deliciously.

Juniper berries also have therapeutic uses, as a diuretic and as a treatment for indigestion and flatulence. Juniper is easy to grow, but it is essential to have both male and female plants to achieve a crop of berries.

recipes using juniper berries, see pages: 133; 135; 205

galangal

Galangal is one of those baffling plants that crops up over the centuries in different countries and under different names. In medieval Britain, where it was known as galingale and was highly esteemed, it was probably the root of a plant called *Cyperus longus*. In the Far East, where it is widely used today, it may be one of two plants, greater or lesser galangal, and its Latin name varies from *Kaempferia* to *Alpinia* to *Languas*.

It is worth knowing some of galangal's Eastern names in order to recognize it in oriental shops. Galangal may be found in three forms: fresh, dried whole and ground. In each of these states it resembles a duller ginger. It is called *laos* and *kencur* in Indonesia; *khaa*, *kha* or *ka* in Thailand; and *langhuas* in Malaysia. In its powdered form it is often called *laos* powder.

Whatever its name, galangal is rarely used today outside Indonesian cuisine. It is not unlike ginger in appearance and flavour: an edible rhizome, duller in colour and with a more complex, earthy taste. It has faint overtones of camphor too, with a not unpleasant musky overlay.

recipe using galangal, see page 189

mace

Mace is the dried outer coating of the seed of the nutmeg tree. It grows in broad bands, called blades, forming a net-like cage around the nutmeg. It is sold either whole, in flattened blades, or ground into powder.

Mace is similar to nutmeg in flavour, but with an added earthy overtone. When fresh, the bands of mace are bright red, but they turn a gingery brown when dried. The blades are used whole in dishes that require long cooking, while the powdered form may be added towards the end of cooking. In the West mace is traditionally used in savoury dishes and nutmeg is more often used in sweet dishes. In India, however, both mace and nutmeg are only ever used in savoury dishes and in spice mixtures like *garam masala*.

The nutmeg tree grew originally in the Molucca Islands and spread to other parts of Indonesia. The trade in nutmeg and mace was controlled first by Arab traders, then by the Portuguese, then the Dutch, and finally by the English. Mace was very highly esteemed in medieval England, more popular even than nutmeg.

recipes using mace, see pages: 135; 137

nutmeg

Nutmeg is the seed of the nutmeg tree. It grows within a lacy cage of mace, inside a fleshy peach-like fruit. It is dried in the sun after harvesting, and is sold both whole and in powdered form. Although very hard to grate, the whole nutmeg may be cracked easily with a hammer. It is best bought whole, as the ground form soon loses its fragrance.

The nutmeg tree grew first in the Molucca Islands and formed a valuable part of the spice trade. It is now widely grown throughout Indonesia and in Grenada. It is a large tree, growing up to 18 m (60 feet) high.

Nutmeg has been popular in Britain since medieval times, usually for flavouring sweet milky dishes like junket and rice pudding. It is also paired with vegetables like onion, cauliflower, spinach and potato; used in milk-based sauces, in spiced fruit cakes and in mulled wine.

recipes using nutmeg, see pages: 95; 189

nigella
nigella sativa

The seed of an otherwise nondescript species of love-in-the-mist, nigella is perhaps better known under its Indian name, kalonji, although it is often (wrongly) sold in Indian shops as black onion seed or even as black cumin seed. Once identified, it is not easily forgotten, for this minuscule, heart-shaped seed in dusty jet black, looking rather like coal dust, is unmistakable. Nigella has a weird, earthy flavour, not exactly agreeable when eaten alone, but good in conjunction with other spices or foods. Its crunchy texture is used to good advantage when the seeds are sprinkled over soft tandoor-baked breads, like naan, before cooking, as is done in northern India. It is also widely used in Bengali spice mixtures and when pickling fish and vegetables. In the countries of the Middle East, nigella seeds, called *shamar* in Arabic, are mixed with sesame seeds and sprinkled on bread rolls before baking. Nigella has therapeutic powers, cleansing the blood of toxins and helping to stimulate the liver. They can be used to treat hepatitis and to improve the complexion.

Nigella sativa is an annual growing 45 cm (18 inches) high and produces blue flowers. It is a native of the eastern Mediterranean, North Africa and the Middle East. Today it grows wild throughout Central Europe and Asia, and is widely cultivated in India and the Middle East.

poppy seeds

The opium poppy, from which the edible seeds are taken, grew first in Asia Minor and has been widely cultivated in Turkey, Iran, India and China. It is a herbaceous annual growing 30 cm–1 m (1–3 feet) tall, with large, pretty, pale flowers. The petals have wavy edges and vary in colour from lilac and pink to white and variegated. The seeds are contained in one large seed pod in the centre of the flower. If the unripe seed pod is cut open, opium oozes out. The ripe seeds, however, are harmless; they contain merely the poppy seed oil, called *huile d'oeillette* or *olivette* in France, which is used by cooks and artists alike.

Although the seeds do not contain opium, both they and the petals have a slight soporific property, and can be made into a syrup to take as a calming agent for coughs and other bronchial troubles. An infusion of the dried petals can be taken at night as a sedative. Alternatively, according to the great herbalist Maurice Mességué, a few of the petals may be added to an infusion of lime flowers, or *tilleul*. The flowers may also be made into a poultice for external use in treating inflammation of the eye or eyelid.

There are two sorts of poppy seed: the more common grey-blue one, and a pale, creamy yellow one, called 'white' poppy seed, which comes from a species of poppy that is grown in India and does not produce opium. The grey seed is used in Central European, Balkan and Slav cookery, and in Jewish cuisine they are sprinkled on bagels, bread rolls, biscuits and cakes. In Russia, the same seeds are usually boiled, then pounded and mixed with honey for use as a filling for cakes and sweet dishes. In India, the white poppy seeds are toasted and then pounded to a paste with a little water and used instead of flour to thicken sauces and curries.

Papaver somniferum is easily grown by sowing in the spring in rich, damp soil in full sun. The seed may be scattered over fine tilth or sown in drills 30 cm (12 inches) apart. If left alone, poppies will self-seed with ease, but if growing them just for their seed, they should be harvested as soon as the petals fall. If the petals are to be used, they must be picked at their peak and spread on paper to dry in a sheltered, shady spot in the open air.

allspice *Pimenta dioica*

Allspice is the berry of an evergreen tree that grows wild in South America and the West Indies. The berries, which are picked and dried before they ripen, have an interesting flavour which resembles a mixture of other spices (hence the name), notably cloves, cinnamon and nutmeg, or mace. Allspice used to be called Jamaica pepper, since this was one of its places of origin. An easy substitute for allspice can be made by mixing equal parts of ground cinnamon and mace and with ½ part each of ground cloves and ground pepper. Or, for savoury dishes like pâtés and terrines, you can use the French mixture *quatre epices*, which is composed of a similar mixture of spices, but this is too peppery for use in sweet dishes.

In Britain, allspice is used in sweet dishes, such as puddings and fruit cakes, whereas in the Middle East, especially in Turkey, it is used predominantly in savoury dishes of rice, game and minced meat.

recipes using allspice, see pages: 135; 175; 194; 195

aniseed

Aniseed, also called anise, is a member of the hemlock family, and dangerously similar to its poisonous relative. The main difference lies in the seeds, which in the case of aniseed are borne in pairs. Aniseed can be raised only from seed, but it is easily grown in a sunny sheltered spot. It grows about 45 cm (18 inches) high and has umbels of tiny white flowers in summer. The seeds are greyish-brown, oval and slightly ridged, and should be gathered in the autumn, unless the plant is to be allowed to self-seed.

Aniseed has a strange, liquorice-like flavour, loved by some and abhorred by others. In the Mediterranean countries it is used to flavour aperitifs like Pernod, anisette, ouzo, raki and arak, while in Central and northern European countries it is used in baking breads and cakes. In South-east Asia and in India it is used in curries, most predominantly with fish.

Aniseed has powerful medicinal properties, mainly as a digestive, a stimulant for a sluggish system and a cure for flatulence. It has been used to these ends in China and India since ancient times. Its digestive powers explain why it is used in so many Mediterranean aperitifs, while in India the seeds are often chewed after a meal, both as a digestive and to sweeten the breath. An effective treatment for indigestion can be made by pouring 1 litre (1¾ pints) boiling water on to 1 teaspoon aniseed, leaving it for about 4–5 minutes, then drinking the aniseed and water mixture three times a day until the condition is alleviated.

cubebs Piper cubeba

A form of pepper now rarely seen outside the East Indies and North Africa, cubebs are the fruit of a perennial vine related to the true pepper vine, *Piper nigrum*. The cubeb vine grows wild in Java and Sumatra. It is often cultivated on coffee plantations, growing in the shade of the coffee bushes. The unripe berries, slightly larger than peppercorns, are dried before use. They are sometimes called 'tailed pepper', as each berry has a stem attached. They have a slightly bitter flavour, halfway between pepper and allspice, and were once used like pepper by the Arabs, who introduced them to Europe. Cubebs were popular in medieval Britain as a flavouring for food and as a medicament, but their use petered out and has never been revived.

Medicinally, cubebs have much the same properties as pepper and may be used ground or an an infusion. They are effective when used as a stimulant or a carminative, and can also be used to treat cystitis and bronchitis.

pepper

Pepper has a fascinating history, as it was one of the first spices to reach the West from the East, and has been one of, if not *the*, most highly valued spices ever since. References to pepper have been found in Greek and Roman writings dating back to the fifth century BC, and it was considered literally worth its weight in gold by the Romans.

Black, white and green peppercorns are the berries of the climbing vine *Piper nigrum*, which grows wild in the tropical forests of Asia. The berries are green before they ripen, when they turn bright red. Black peppercorns are the unripe berries that have been picked by hand and left to dry in the sun, whereupon they shrivel up, harden and turn dark brown. White peppercorns are allowed to ripen on the vine before they are picked, also by hand, soaked and milled to remove the outer skin. White peppercorns lack the aromatic quality of black pepper; their only virtue seems to be for fussy cooks who object to the look of black specks in pale dishes. I have never minded this, and find little use for them. Both black and white pepper are best used freshly ground, for they soon lose their aromatic qualities.

Green peppercorns are also picked before they ripen and then are freeze-dried, pickled or simply preserved in cans or jars. They can sometimes be bought fresh, still on the stem and are soft enough to be squashed between the fingers. They have a mild, fresh, sappy taste.

Pink peppercorns are the berries of an unrelated South American plant, *schinus molle*. None the less, they have a definite taste of pepper, although milder and sweeter than the real thing. Their advantage, which has made them popular, is their visual appeal. They are often sold mixed with green and black peppercorns, and are used mainly for colour contrast.

Pepper also has its uses in promoting health. Taken ground, as a powder, it acts as a stimulant and a carminative, and has febrifugal powers. It is also effective as a digestive, to treat flatulence, and as a diuretic. Pepper has one disadvantage: it can cause congestion of the blood vessels, and therefore its use should be avoided, or minimized, by people suffering from varicose veins or haemorrhoids.

recipes using pepper, see pages: 96; 129; 130; 133; 135; 141; 166; 177; 178; 189; 194; 195

mastic

This is a strange substance not much seen outside the Middle East and the Balkans. Formed naturally from the resinous sap of the low-growing, bushy, evergreen *lentisk* tree, it looks for all the world like candy: irregular lumps of pale amber-coloured crystal. It is often chewed with a piece of wax, like chewing gum, when it gives off an aromatic taste, like that obtained from pine needles. The gum has a strange, smoky flavour. Its main use lies in flavouring sweet dishes, such as Greek rice pudding and Turkish delight. It must be pounded or crushed before use, usually in conjunction with sugar and rosewater. The *lentisk* tree, a species of pine tree, grows wild in Greece, Turkey and the Middle East, especially on the Greek island of Chios, which exports mastic in large quantities.

The sap of the tree is poisonous and the branches should be handled with care, for some people are highly allergic to them, even to their touch. A substance obtained from the leaves is used to tan and dye leather.

sumac

Sumac is made from the dried berries of a large shrub that grows in temperate regions throughout the Middle East and around the Mediterranean. The shrub grows 1–3 m (3–10 feet) high, and has greenish-white flowers borne in panicles in July and August. These are followed by small red berries which ripen slowly. Just before the berries are ripe, the boughs are cut and the berries left to dry on the branches in the sun. The dried berries are ground into a coarse red powder, the colour of dried blood, which has a pleasantly sour taste, like salt and lemon juice combined. The powder is used as a spice in Iran, Iraq, Turkey and most of the Middle Eastern countries, especially Lebanon.

Sumac is used mainly in salad dressings and in marinades for fish, chicken and meat. It is used in much the same way as lemon juice. It is also one of the three ingredients, with wild thyme and sesame seeds, in the Middle Eastern spice mixture called *za'atar*.

Sesamum indicum
sesame seeds

Sesame is an annual, growing 60–90 cm (2–3 feet) high, with pale pink or white flowers. It grows wild in Morocco and India; in colder climates it is best grown under glass, in a heated greenhouse or conservatory. The seed of an annual plant, available in three colours: pearly white, cream and black. The last is rarely seen in the West, except in oriental shops, but is very popular in Japan. Of all the seeds, I find sesame the most delicious, almost addictive. They are also one of the most nutritious, being rich in vitamins and minerals – and very high in calories.

Sesame seeds are ground into two oils, both useful in different ways. One is a light, refined oil, almost flavourless, good for frying and dressing light salads. The other is a rich, complex oil, dense in flavour, made with the toasted seeds. This is very concentrated and only a few drops are needed. It is much used as a flavouring in China and Japan.

In the Middle East, sesame seeds are ground into tahini, an oily paste rather like a smooth, thin peanut butter. Nutritious and fattening, tahini is used as the basis of many delicious oily spreads such as hummus, made with chickpeas, and *baba ghannouj*, made with roasted aubergines.

Like most seeds, sesame seeds are greatly enhanced by a preliminary roasting in a dry frying pan over gentle heat for 2–3 minutes. They can then be scattered over salads, cooked vegetables or – almost best of all – thick slices of brown bread and butter.

recipes using sesame seeds, see pages: 115; 160

mustard seeds

There are three basic mustard seeds: white (*Sinapsis alba*), which is also called yellow; brown (*Brassica juncea*), which is also called oriental; and black (*B. nigra*). Brown mustard comes in two forms, one with a light brown coat, and the other with a black coat. True black mustard is rarely seen anymore and has been replaced by brown mustard. Both black and white mustard grew first in southern Europe, while brown mustard is a native of India.

English mustard is made with a combination of brown, with a light brown coat, and white mustard seeds. The combination of the two seeds is vital; the white mustard gives heat on the tongue, the brown mustard gives a volatile heat at the back of the throat, like curry powder, making the eyes water. English is the hottest of all the mustards. The strength varies slightly from year to year, depending on the weather and the country of origin. English mustard also differs from other mustards in that it is sold dry as well as mixed to a paste, to be mixed to a paste with cold water, thus keeping its fiery strength indefinitely. (Prepared mustards lose some heat each time they are exposed to the air.)

French mustard is made mainly in and around Dijon, Bordeaux and Meaux, not far from Paris. The best known of these outside France is Dijon mustard, which is made from brown mustard seeds only, mixed with white wine and spices. This is milder than English mustard. A wholegrain mustard, often called *à l'ancienne*, has recently been revived and is very popular. One of the best known is made at Meaux.

Mustard's force is invalidated by heat, which destroys the enzymes. For this reason, dry mustard must always be mixed with cold water. For the same reason, mustard can be added in fairly generous quantities to a cooked sauce or casserole without overheating it, yet retaining the flavour. The enzyme activity is also hindered by mixing with acids, such as vinegar, lemon juice and wine.

recipes using mustard seeds, see pages: 141; 162; 165; 182

tamarind Tamarindus indica

The tamarind is a graceful tree which grows to about 12–18 m (40–60 feet) tall. Its origins are unknown, but it has been cultivated in India for centuries. It was known in Britain in medieval times, and was taken to the West Indies by the Spaniards in the sixteenth and seventeenth centuries. It is now cultivated widely in India, and in the East and West Indies.

The tree is an evergreen, with light green leaves and yellow flowers striped with red. These are followed by light brown, hairy pods 7–15 cm (3–6 inches) long and 2.5 cm (1 inch) wide, looking like fat broad bean pods. Each pod contains 4–10 seeds, which are surrounded by a sticky dark red paste with fibrous strings.

Tamarind can be bought in three forms: fresh, still in the pods; in rectangular blocks of sticky pulp, seeds and fibres, semi-dried and compressed; and as a concentrate, a thick, dark red purée. To make tamarind water, simply break off the brittle shells, pull away the fibrous threads and pour boiling water over the contents of the pods. Leave to cool, then, using the fingers, pull away the pulp and discard the seeds. Push the pulp through a small food mill or coarse sieve, using a little of the soaking water to help it through.

To use the compressed form, break off as much as you need and put it in a bowl. Cover it with hot water, then leave it for about 1 hour. Loosen the pulp by pulling and squeezing, and push it through a coarse sieve, using a little of the soaking water to moisten it.

To use the concentrate, dilute as much as you need with a little hot water. This is certainly the quickest and simplest form to use, but it is not always available in the shops.

In India, tamarind is prized for its medicinal properties. It is used to treat upsets of the stomach and bowels, and as a laxative, astringent, febrifuge and natural antiseptic. The leaves are used, boiled down to an essence, to treat jaundice and dysentery.

recipes using tamarind, see pages: 130; 202

fenugreek

Fenugreek is an annual, a member of the pea and clover family, which bears its seeds in tiny pods. It has small, pale yellow flowers. Fenugreek seeds are small, dusty yellow and almost square. They are rock hard and must be ground before use. Fenugreek is usually roasted before grinding, otherwise the seeds are almost tasteless, but the roasting must be gentle or the seeds will become bitter. They may also be sprouted, like mung beans, and eaten raw in salads; treated in this way they are extra nutritious, for during the process of germination the vitamin B and C content increases considerably, as does the enzyme content. Sprouted fenugreek is also a valuable source of protein and has effective antiscorbutic properties.

Much used in Indian cookery, fenugreek is a basic ingredient of curry powder, although it does not figure in *garam masala*, possibly because it needs long cooking to bring out its flavour, and *garam masala* is often added only at the end of the cooking time. Fenugreek is used in dishes of fish, meat and vegetables in Indian cuisine, and in bread in North Africa.

The leaves are also used, both fresh and dried, in Indian cookery; they have a slightly bitter taste. They are sometimes found, called *methi*, in Indian shops. Fenugreek is easily grown from seed, so long as the seed is relatively fresh.

Medicinally, fenugreek has many functions. It acts as a digestive and as a stimulant, and is thought to encourage the appetite. For this reason it was popular with Egyptian men, who encouraged their womenfolk to eat lots of it, as they liked them to be fat.

wasabi Wasabia japonica

Although known in the West as Japanese horseradish, wasabi is unrelated to true horseradish (*Armoracia rusticana*). Wasabi is a perennial plant, which grows, rather like watercress, on the marshy edges of rivers and streams. The light green rhizomes are eaten very finely grated. They have a delicious, hot, sharp, fresh taste, like a cross between horseradish and English mustard. In Japan, special graters, finer than any European or American grater, are made for grating wasabi and ginger. They are produced in three or four sizes, in copper coated with tin, and shaped like small, flat spades. These graters have tiny triangular spikes facing two ways, which reduce the root to a fine juicy pulp.

Wasabi is always served with sashimi, the superlative Japanese raw fish dish, and moulded sushi topped with sashimi; it is piled on the side of the plate in a little cone like a miniature Mount Fuji. Together with a dipping sauce made with soy sauce and mirin, this sets off the delicate flavour of the raw fish to perfection. (A little of the grated wasabi is sometimes stirred into the dipping sauce by each diner.)

The root itself cannot be bought in the West, alas, but wasabi can be found in Japanese shops in two forms: powdered, in small cans; and as a paste, in tubes. The powdered wasabi must be mixed, like mustard, with a little warm water; the prepared paste is used as it comes from the tube.

It is not practicable to grow wasabi, since the difficulty of finding a source of clean running water is almost as great as that of finding the root to plant outside Japan.

recipe using wasabi, see page 121

Szechuan pepper

Also called anise pepper and *fagara*, Szechuan pepper is made from the seed casings of a species of prickly ash that grows wild in China. The reddish-brown berries are picked in the autumn and left to dry in the sun; when the casings burst open, the small black seeds inside are discarded, for they have a bitter taste. The chestnut brown seed casings are then roasted and ground for use as a food flavouring much used in the province of Szechuan. It is one of the ingredients of Chinese five spice powder.

This semi-hardy deciduous species of ash grows about 3 m (10 feet) high, with sharp prickles and small white flowers borne in panicles.

Both bark and berries have been used medicinally for centuries. The bark is crushed or powdered and used as a compress for healing wounds, toothache and headaches. The berries are used in the form of an infusion; they are antispasmodic as well as carminative, good for treating dyspepsia and indigestion. They also cause perspiration, thus reducing fevers, as well as acting as a stimulant in helping the circulation of the blood and banishing lethargy. (For more information, see also sansho, page 88.)

sansho

Zanthoxylum piperitum, Fagara piperitum

This is the Japanese form of Szechuan pepper (see page 87), sometimes called Japanese pepper. It is made from the dried seed casings of the same prickly ash tree as the Chinese variety. In Japan, sansho is considered to be an aid to the digestion of rich and fatty foods, and is always served as accompaniment to grilled eel. In small, old-fashioned restaurants in Tokyo that specialize in this delicacy, sansho is served in a shaker and offered with the strips of grilled eel arranged on a bed of rice, in a rectangular red lacquer box with a tiny dish of pickles and some thin strips of nori (dried seaweed). Sansho has a most unusual taste, rather like a cross between lemon grass and black pepper. It has the same strange, slightly numbing effect on the tongue as Szechuan pepper. The Japanese also serve it with chicken and duck. In spring the young leaves of the prickly ash, called *kimone*, are picked and used as a garnish for many Japanese dishes; they are also used to flavour vinegar.

Zingiber officinale

ginger

Ginger is an ancient plant, used in China both as a flavouring for food and as a medicament since the sixth century BC. It grows wild in South-east Asia, China and Japan. Today India, west Africa and the West Indies are the largest growers of ginger for export. It is a perennial, whose leafy stems grow roughly 1 m (3 feet) tall, from rhizomes lying just below the surface of the soil. The rhizomes are the edible part, and are used fresh, dried, pickled or preserved in syrup.

Ginger may be grown from a 5 cm (2 inch) piece of rhizome, as long as it has a couple of buds. It should be planted 5 cm (2 inches) deep in rich compost, either in a greenhouse or indoors as a house plant. However, it will produce the large, fleshy rhizomes used for culinary purposes only when grown in a tropical climate.

Ginger is aromatic, therapeutic and immensely effective used either as a medicament or as a flavouring. In the East it is used in baths for toning up the system and for relieving muscular aches and pains. It is taken internally as a digestive and to warm up the whole body. In Tudor England it was held to be an aphrodisiac.

Fresh ginger is usually classified as a food flavouring, being neither a herb nor a spice, so for the purposes of this book we are dealing with ginger in its dried, ground form: the golden brown, aromatic powder that has been a favourite spice in northern Europe since Roman times. In medieval France and England spiced gingerbread, like *pain d'epice*, was gilded with gold leaf and tooled like leather. In Thomas Hardy's England spiced gingerbread and ginger biscuits were traditional 'fairings', bought by young men at country fairs to give to their girlfriends.

Ginger wine, an excellent cold-weather drink, has been manufactured in Britain since the first half of the eighteenth century, and is still available today. Drunk with whisky, it has long been a favourite of mine, a last resort in time of chill, exhaustion or depression. Ginger beer is another old-fashioned drink that is still popular. This was our Sunday lunchtime treat as children; luckily, our parents did not seem to be aware of its alcohol content.

recipes using ginger, see pages: 95; 116; 121; 129; 130; 132; 133; 136; 172; 175; 189; 191; 195; 196 **89**

recipe section
90–205

celery soup
with lovage and chives

1 large head celery, inner sticks and leaves only

40 g (1½ oz) butter

500 g (1 lb) potatoes, peeled and thickly sliced

1½ tablespoons roughly chopped lovage

1.2 litres (2 pints) chicken stock, heated

salt and black pepper

Garnish:

150 ml (¼ pint) single cream

1½ tablespoons chopped chives

Serves 6

1. Chop the celery, reserving the leaves. Cook the celery in the butter for 5 minutes, then add the potatoes and lovage, and stir for a further 3–4 minutes.

2. Pour in the heated stock, add salt and pepper, and bring to the boil. Reduce the heat, cover the pan and simmer the soup gently for 35 minutes. Remove from the heat and leave to cool.

3. Purée the soup in a liquidizer or food processor, or push through a medium food mill, then return to a clean pan and reheat gently. Chop the reserved celery leaves finely. Pour the warm soup into bowls and garnish each one with a swirl of cream and 1 teaspoon each of chopped celery leaves and chives.

herb and spice information: celery leaves p16; lovage p29; chives P12

spinach soup
with nutmeg or ginger

herb and spice information: nutmeg p73; ginger p89

150 g (5 oz) onion, finely chopped

25 g (1 oz) butter

1 tablespoon sunflower oil

250 g (8 oz) spinach

150 g (5 oz) potato, peeled and diced

900 ml (1½ pints) chicken stock, heated

sea salt and black pepper

Garnish:

6 tablespoons cream (any thickness) or 6 tablespoons yogurt

freshly grated nutmeg or ground ginger

Serves 4

1. Cook the chopped onion in the butter and sunflower oil for 5 minutes, then add the spinach and cook for another 5 minutes. Add the diced potato and cook for 3–4 minutes, stirring.

2. Pour on the heated stock and bring to the boil. Add salt and pepper to taste, partly cover the pan and cook gently for 25 minutes. Then cool for a little while before puréeing in a food processor.

3. To serve the soup, reheat it and pour into individual bowls. Swirl cream or yogurt into each portion and then sprinkle with a little freshly grated nutmeg or ground ginger.

fish soup
with herbs

1½ tablespoons olive oil

25 g (1 oz) butter

1 small onion, chopped

1 leek, chopped

1 carrot, chopped

1 celery stick, chopped

1 garlic clove, chopped

2 tomatoes, chopped

1 small bay leaf, crumbled

½ tablespoon dried *herbes de Provence*

1–1.25 kg (2–2½ lb) mixed white fish: grey mullet, monkfish, conger eel, cut into bite-sized pieces

4 tablespoons Pernod or vodka

⅛ teaspoon saffron threads

1 tablespoon chopped marjoram

1 tablespoon chopped thyme

½ teaspoon crushed red peppercorns

salt and pepper

6 slices French bread

Serves 6

1. Heat the oil and butter in a deep pan and brown the chopped onion, leek, carrot and celery. After 3 minutes, add the garlic and tomatoes, then the crumbled bay leaf, dried herbs, salt and pepper. After another 3 minutes, put in the pieces of fish, stirring well to mix them with the vegetables and dried herbs. Pour on the Pernod or vodka, and continue to cook gently for another 2–3 minutes, stirring. Add 1 litre (1¾ pints) very hot water and bring slowly to the boil. Cover the pan and simmer slowly for 1 hour.

2. Meanwhile, dry the French bread slices under a low grill or in a cool oven until crisp, but not browned. Cool on a wire rack. Towards the end of the cooking time, tip the saffron into a small bowl and pour a couple of spoonfuls of the hot fish stock over it, then leave to infuse.

3. Leave the soup to cool for a little while, then pick out and discard the big, bony pieces of fish. Save some of the best pieces of fish for later, and push the rest of the soup through a coarse sieve or food mill, mashing the remaining pieces of fish and the vegetables against the sides.

4. Tip into a clean pan and reheat, adding the saffron infusion and more salt and pepper to taste. Flake the reserved fish, discarding skin and bone, and add it to the soup with the marjoram, thyme and crushed red peppercorns.

5. Spoon the soup into bowls, and garnish each one with a slice of French bread. Serve at once.

herb and spice information: garlic p11; bay leaves p27; herbes de Provence P49; saffron p61; marjoram p34; thyme p47; red peppercorns p79

black bean soup
with coriander

500 g (1 lb) dried black (or red) kidney beans

1 large red onion, finely chopped

3 tablespoons light olive oil

3 large garlic cloves, finely chopped

3 red chillies, deseeded and finely chopped

2 tablespoons tomato purée

600 ml (1 pint) chicken or vegetable stock, heated

a pinch of cayenne

1½ tablespoons lime juice

salt and black pepper

Garnish:

6–8 tablespoons Bourbon whisky (optional)

150 ml (¼ pint) crème fraîche or soured cream

3–4 tablespoons chopped coriander leaves

Serves 6 to 8

This delicious soup is based on one of Frances Bissell's recipes, with my variations and her consent. It can be made with red kidney beans if black ones are hard to find. Start preparation 1 day in advance.

1. Cover the dried beans generously with cold water and soak for 8 hours or overnight. Then drain them and cover with fresh cold water. Do not add salt at this stage. Bring to the boil and boil hard for 10 minutes, then reduce the heat and simmer gently for 50 minutes or until the beans are soft. Leave to cool in their liquid for about 1 hour.

2. Drain the beans in a colander standing over a large bowl. Reserve about 500 g (1 lb) of the cooked beans, and purée the rest in a food processor with 600 ml (1 pint) of their cooking liquid. Alternatively, push the cooked beans and measured liquid through a coarse food mill. Reserve the rest of the bean stock in case it is required later.

3. Fry the onion gently in the oil for 5–6 minutes. Add the garlic and chillies, and cook for another 2–3 minutes, stirring often to make sure they do not stick. Then add the tomato purée and cook for a further 4–5 minutes, stirring as before. Pour in the heated stock, bring to the boil and simmer for 30 minutes. Stir in the puréed beans, the reserved whole beans, cayenne and salt and pepper to taste. If the soup is too thick, add a little of the reserved bean cooking liquid to thin it. Stir in the lime juice. If possible, leave the soup to stand for a few hours and reheat before serving.

4. To serve, ladle the soup into bowls, adding a dash of Bourbon, for those who like it, a dollop of crème fraîche or soured cream, and sprinkle with coriander. Alternatively, serve the soup quite plain, adding Bourbon for those who wish, and hand around the cream and coriander at the table.

herb and spice information: garlic p11; chillies p56; cayenne p55; coriander leaves p22

consommé with mixed vegetables

1.2 litres (2 pints) chicken stock

125 g (4 oz) carrot, diced

125 g (4 oz) leek, diced

125 g (4 oz) cooked beetroot, peeled and diced

125 g (4 oz) courgettes, diced

125 g (4 oz) yellow or red pepper, diced

1 red or green chilli, deseeded and finely chopped

50 g (2 oz) shelled peas

sea salt and black pepper

4 tablespoons chopped chervil, to garnish

Serves 6

This soup is also excellent served chilled in hot weather. It may be eaten quite plain, with chopped chervil, or with a spoonful of yogurt added to each bowl and the chervil sprinkled over it.

1. Put the stock in a pan and add the carrot, leek and beetroot. Bring slowly to the boil and simmer for 10 minutes, then add the courgettes, pepper and chilli. Bring back to the boil and simmer for another 10 minutes, then add the peas and simmer again for 4–5 minutes, adding salt and pepper to taste. Serve hot, in bowls, liberally sprinkled with chopped chervil.

herb and spice information: chilli p56; chervil p15

fish soup with rouille

1 kg (2 lb) mixed white fish: monkfish, grey mullet, conger eel, cod, and so on, with their bones

1 onion, halved

1 carrot, halved

1 celery stick, halved

1 bay leaf

2 tablespoons olive oil

1 leek, sliced

1 garlic clove, finely chopped

2 tomatoes, skinned and finely chopped

2 sprigs fennel

5 cm (2 inch) strip orange peel

½ teaspoon powdered saffron

¼ teaspoon cayenne

2–3 dashes Tabasco Sauce

salt and black pepper

Garnish:

18 thin slices French bread, dried in the oven

Rouille (see page 187)

freshly grated Parmesan cheese

Serves 6

1. Fillet the fish and put the bones in a deep pot with the onion, carrot and celery. Cover with 1.5 litres (2½ pints) water, adding the bay leaf, salt and pepper. Bring to the boil slowly, skimming as it nears boiling point. Half cover the pan and boil gently for 30 minutes, then strain and reserve the stock, discard the bones and vegetables.

2. Heat the oil in a pan and cook the leek for 3 minutes. Add the garlic and cook for 2 minutes, add the tomatoes and cook for another 2 minutes. Bury the fennel and orange peel in the vegetables.

3. Divide the fish into firm fillets (such as monkfish and conger eel) and softer fish (like grey mullet). Cut into small pieces and lay the firmer fish on top of the vegetables. Cover the pan and cook gently for 4 minutes, then add the fish stock. Bring to the boil and cook briskly for 10 minutes. Reduce the heat, add the softer fish and simmer for 5 minutes. Turn off the heat, add the saffron, cayenne and Tabasco. Let stand, covered, for 5–10 minutes before serving.

4. To serve, pour into a large tureen or individual soup bowls. Place dishes of dried bread, rouille and freshly grated Parmesan on the table. Each person then spreads the rouille or the grated cheese on the bread and floats it in the soup.

Note: If using saffron threads, toast them first by holding them in a large metal spoon over a low heat for 30 seconds, then pound in a mortar. Pour 2 tablespoons boiling water over the pounded saffron and leave for 10 minutes to infuse. Then add to the soup along with the cayenne and Tabasco.

Danish egg cake
with chives

1 tablespoon plain flour

75 ml (3 fl oz) milk

4 eggs, beaten

15 g (½ oz) butter

4 tablespoons chopped chives

salt and black pepper

6–8 bacon rashers, grilled,
to garnish

Serves 2

*Serve a green salad to accompany this plain
omelette; grilled tomatoes also go well with this
simple dish*

1. Using a wire whisk, whisk the flour into the milk,
then gradually add the beaten eggs, continuing to
whisk. Season with salt and black pepper to taste
while whisking.

2. Heat the butter in a frying pan. When it is hot,
pour in the beaten eggs and cook quickly until set, as
for an omelette, tilting the pan from side to side and
lifting the edge of the omelette to allow the liquid
egg to run underneath.

3. Slide the set egg on to a flat dish and scatter the
chopped chives thickly over the top. Garnish with
grilled bacon rashers.

herb and spice information: chives P12

Danish custard
with leeks and garlic

25 g (1 oz) butter

1 tablespoon sunflower oil

1 leek, very finely chopped

2 garlic cloves, very finely chopped

6 eggs

600 ml (1 pint) chicken stock

2½ tablespoons chopped chervil

salt and black pepper

75 g (3 oz) mâche or rocket,
to garnish

Serves 6

1. Heat the butter and oil in a frying pan and cook the chopped leek for 3 minutes, then add the garlic and cook for another minute. Set the pan aside.

2. Break the eggs into a bowl and add salt and pepper to taste. Stir in the leek and garlic mixture, then the chicken stock. Lastly, add 1½ tablespoons of the chopped chervil and mix well. Thoroughly butter 6 small soufflé or *cocotte* dishes and pour in the custard. Stand them in a broad flameproof casserole and pour in enough water to come halfway up their sides. Bring to the boil, reduce the heat and cover the casserole. Cook gently for 12–14 minutes, taking care that the water does not boil up over the sides of the custard dishes.

3. When the custards are set, remove them from the casserole and leave them to stand for 5 minutes, covered. Arrange the mâche or rocket on small plates. Run a small knife around the edge of each custard and turn each out on a plate of salad leaves. Sprinkle the rest of the chopped chervil over the custards and serve immediately. These custards are also good served cold.

herb and spice information: garlic p11; chervil p15; rocket p24

eggs on spinach
with watercress sauce

Watercress Sauce (see page 181)

1 kg (2 lb) spinach

4 eggs

Serves 4
as a first course or light main dish.

1. Have the watercress sauce already made and keeping warm over hot water. Drop the spinach into some lightly salted boiling water and cook for 4–5 minutes, depending on whether it is summer or winter spinach. Drain it well in a colander, pressing out the water with the back of a wooden spoon. Then divide it equally between 4 bowls.

2. Lower the eggs into boiling water and cook for exactly 5 minutes. Cool for a few moments in a bowl of cold water, then shell them and lay one egg in each bowl of spinach. Pour the watercress sauce on top and serve as soon as possible.

herb and spice information: watercress p32

eggs in coriander mayonnaise

8 eggs

2 Little Gem lettuces

500 g (1 lb) cooked peeled prawns or 250 g (8 oz) white crabmeat, flaked

300 ml (½ pint) soured cream

300 ml (½ pint) mayonnaise

2 tablespoons finely chopped coriander leaves

Serves 4
as a first course.

1. Drop the eggs into lightly salted boiling water and cook for 8 minutes. Transfer them to a bowl of cold water, then shell them carefully.

2. Separate the lettuces into leaves, and lay them on a shallow dish. Lay the whole eggs over them, then scatter the prawns or flaked crabmeat over and among them.

3. Mix the soured cream with the mayonnaise, then stir in the chopped coriander, keeping back a little for the garnish. Spread the mayonnaise mixture over the dish and scatter the reserved coriander over all. Chill for 1–2 hours before serving.

egg mayonnaise
on spinach

Chilli Mayonnaise (see page 183)

6 eggs

1 kg (2 lb) spinach

sea salt and black pepper

Serves 4
as a fairly substantial first course.

A chilli-accented mayonnaise makes a good contrast to the bland eggs, lifting this excellent dish out of the ordinary.

1. Make the chilli mayonnaise as instructed. Boil the eggs in salted water for 12 minutes, then cool in a bowl of cold water. Place the spinach in a large pan of lightly salted boiling water and cook for 4–5 minutes, depending on whether it is tender summer or coarser winter spinach. Drain very well, squeezing out all the moisture in a colander with the back of a wooden spoon.

2. Make a bed of spinach, still slightly warm, on a flat platter, seasoning it with sea salt and black pepper. Shell the eggs, cut them in half and place them on the spinach, then spoon the mayonnaise over all. Serve soon after making.

scrambled eggs
with green chillies

Green chillies bring a fresh, spicy flavour to creamy scrambled eggs, served on rich tomato toast. Serve these as a light meal, with a green salad to refresh the palate.

4 slices wholemeal bread

50 g (2 oz) butter

2 tablespoons tomato purée

2 green chillies, deseeded and cut in thin strips

8 eggs, beaten

sea salt and black pepper

handful chives, to garnish

Serves 4

1. Toast the bread, and then butter it lightly, using half the butter. Spread each slice of bread with ½ tablespoon tomato purée, then keep warm.

2. Melt the remaining butter in a frying pan, add the chillies and cook for 30 seconds, stirring. Then tip in the seasoned, beaten eggs and cook gently, stirring continuously, until they are creamy and lightly set. Pile on to the toast to serve and garnish with chives.

herb and spice information: chives p12; chillies p56

fried eggs on sun-dried tomato purée

4 rounds Polenta (see note below)

1 dried chilli, deseeded and stalk removed

6 tablespoons sun-dried tomato paste

4 eggs

butter for frying

sea salt and black pepper

Serves 4
with a green salad.

Provided you have some polenta already cooked and some sun-dried tomato paste to hand, this is a simple and very delicious snack.

1. Have the polenta cut in neat circles or squares about 1 cm (½ inch) thick. Cover the dried chilli with 4 tablespoons boiling water and leave for 20 minutes. Then lift out the chilli and chop; purée with half the soaking water in a small mill or coffee grinder. Stir into the sun-dried tomato paste and mix well.

2. Grill the polenta on a ridged cast-iron grill pan on top of the heat until nicely striped with brown. Alternatively, cook under the grill. Lay the polenta on individual plates and top with the tomato and chilli paste. Keep them warm while you fry the eggs in the butter. Place 1 egg on each prepared plate and serve at once.

Note: To make polenta, bring 600 ml (1 pint) water to the boil in a heavy-based saucepan. Gradually sprinkle in 150 g (5 oz) instant polenta, stirring continuously. When the polenta starts to boil, reduce the heat and simmer gently for 5 minutes. Stir often until the polenta is thick and smooth. When the mixture begins to come away from the side of the pan it is ready. Rinse a baking sheet with cold water and tip the polenta out on to it. Spread the polenta out to 1–1.5 cm (½–¾ inch) thick and leave until cold and firm. Cut into squares or rounds.

herb and spice information: chillies p56

grilled fish with coriander

16 small squid, cleaned

2 tablespoons sunflower oil

1 egg white, lightly beaten

4 tablespoons sesame seeds

salt and black pepper

Garnish:

1 tablespoon sunflower oil

12 sprigs coriander

2 lemons, cut in quarters

Watercress Sauce (see page 181, optional)

Serves 4 as a first course.

1. If the squid have not already been cleaned, proceed as follows. Pull the head, with tentacles attached, out of the body sac. Cut across the head just above the eyes, discarding everything that falls below that line. Open out the tentacles, squeeze out the central polyp and discard it. Wash the body sac under cold running water; pull out the central transparent 'quill' or 'pen' and discard, together with any odd bits and pieces within the sac. If there is an ink sac, discard this also, as ink is not required for this recipe. Wash the body well, inside and out, and pull off the outer skin. Cut off the triangular fins and discard. Chop the tentacles and set aside.

2. Slit each body sac in half and score the outer sides in a diagonal criss-cross pattern, using the point of a sharp knife. Rub them on both sides with sunflower oil. Thread the clumps of tentacles on skewers, then rub them with more oil. Sprinkle all the squid parts with salt and pepper, then lay them on the grill pan. Brush the top surfaces with the lightly beaten egg white, then scatter the sesame seeds on top. Grill for 1½ minutes under a fierce heat, then turn them over and grill the second side for 1½ minutes.

3. While the squid are grilling, prepare the garnish. Heat the sunflower oil in a small frying pan. When it is very hot, throw in the coriander and fry for 30 seconds, turning over and over, then lift out on to kitchen paper to drain.

4. To serve, lay the squid sacs on a flat dish, take the tentacles off the skewers and add them to the dish, then lay the fried coriander sprigs over and around them. Serve the lemon quarters and watercress sauce, if using, separately.

steamed prawns
with ginger and lemon grass

1 tablespoon sesame oil

about 500 g (1 lb) large uncooked
prawns, or 4–6 per person,
depending on size, shells removed
except for tails

8 spring onions, sliced

1 garlic clove, finely chopped

25 g (1 oz) fresh root ginger,
finely chopped

1 stalk lemon grass, cut in 4 and
lightly crushed, or 1 tablespoon
chopped lemon balm

2 teaspoons soy sauce

sea salt and black pepper

1½ tablespoons finely chopped
coriander leaves, to garnish

Serves 4
as a first course or a light
main dish.

*This dish should be made with large uncooked
prawns. The freshwater king prawns are probably the
best, but the stripy saltwater tiger prawns also work
well. I always shell them, leaving only the tails,
before cooking, as it is a messy business trying to
shell them on the plate in a sauce. But some of my
friends do not mind doing that, and prefer to leave
the shells on until the last moment. If you want to
serve them in the shells, allow 1 extra minute
steaming. If serving as a main dish, accompany with
a bowl of plain boiled basmati rice.*

1. Cut 4 pieces of foil about 15 cm (6 inches) square,
and rub each with a few drops of sesame oil. Divide
the prawns evenly between them, and sprinkle with
the sliced spring onions, chopped garlic and ginger.
Lay a piece of lemon grass, or some of the chopped
lemon balm, in the centre of each pile, sprinkle with
salt and pepper and soy sauce. Wrap up the foil
parcels and seal the edges by pinching together.

2. Steam the parcels for 4–6 minutes over boiling
water. If the parcels are very close together with
little room for the steam to circulate, allow an extra
1–2 minutes steaming.

3. Unwrap each package and slide the contents on to
a warm plate. Discard the lemon grass and garnish
with chopped coriander. Serve immediately.

Note: The little packages may be prepared in
advance and kept in the refrigerator for 2–3 hours.

herb and spice information: spring onions p10; garlic p11; ginger p89; lemon grass p23; lemon balm p30;
coriander leaves p22

1. Thoroughly scrub the mussels in cold water and pull off the small bunch of black hairs (known as the beard) from each shell. Discard any open mussels that do not close tightly when tapped.

2. Warm the cream in a small pan. Shake in the saffron and heat almost to boiling point, then remove from the heat and cover the pan.

3. Melt the butter in a deep pot, then add the shallot, parsley and celery leaves, and cook gently for 4 minutes. Tip the mussels into the pot, add the wine and bring to the boil quickly. Then cover the pan and cook for 3–5 minutes, until the mussels have opened. Lift out the mussels and keep warm in a large bowl or soup tureen. Discard any mussels that have not opened.

4. Strain the cooking liquid into a clean pan and reheat. Pour the saffron-infused cream through a small strainer into the mussel stock. Boil all together for a moment, then pour over the mussels and sprinkle with chopped coriander or parsley.

2 kg (4 lb) mussels

150 ml (¼ pint) double cream

¼ teaspoon saffron

15 g (½ oz) butter

1 shallot, chopped

3 stalks parsley, chopped

6 large celery leaves, chopped

300 ml (½ pint) dry white wine

2 tablespoons chopped coriander leaves or flat-leaf parsley, to garnish

Serves 4

herb and spice information: saffron p61; parsley p36; celery leaves p16; coriander leaves p22

moules à la crème
au safran

smoked salmon
with new potatoes and dill

750 g (1½ lb) new potatoes

3 tablespoons virgin olive oil

1 tablespoon white wine vinegar

4 tablespoons chopped dill

500 g (1 lb) smoked salmon, thinly sliced

black pepper

Serves 4
as a light main course.

This is a useful way of transforming smoked salmon into a light main course. Chives may be used instead of dill, if preferred. It is important to get a really good waxy new potato; the best varieties for this are Jersey, Royal, Belle de Fontenay and La Ratte. Serve with buttered rye bread and a green salad to follow.

1. Boil the potatoes in their skins, then drain in a colander. As soon as they are cool enough to handle, peel them and cut into thick slices. Put them in a bowl and add the olive oil, vinegar and black pepper, mixing very gently so as not to break up the potatoes. Lastly, stir in half of the chopped dill.

2. Shortly before serving (the potatoes should still be warm), arrange the smoked salmon on 4 large plates, covering one half of each plate. Lay the potato salad on the other half of each plate and scatter the reserved dill over all.

herb and spice information: dill p13

lobster rolls
with wasabi and ginger

75 g (3 oz) or 2 bunches spring onions

2 tablespoons sunflower oil

1 garlic clove, finely chopped

2 teaspoons grated fresh root ginger

125 g (4 oz) head fennel, shredded

125 g (4 oz) leek, shredded

chopped meat from 500 g (1 lb) lobster

a dash of Maggi or light soy sauce

about 75 g (3 oz) filo pastry

40 g (1½ oz) butter, melted

Wasabi and Ginger Sauce:

4 tablespoons sake or dry vermouth

4 tablespoons light soy sauce

½ teaspoon wasabi

½ teaspoon grated fresh root ginger

Serves 4

1. Trim the spring onions down to 3.5 cm (1½ inches) in length and cut them lengthways into thin slivers. Heat a wok or deep pan, then add and heat the oil. When the oil is very hot, put in the spring onions and toss for 1 minute, then add the garlic and ginger. Toss together for 1 minute, then add the fennel and leek and toss for another 1–2 minutes. Now put the chopped lobster into the pan and add the Maggi or soy sauce. Toss again for 1 minute, then set aside.

2. Unfold the filo and spread out 1 sheet, keeping the others loosely covered with a damp cloth. Cut the first sheet into 15 x 25 cm (6 x 10 inch) strips. Brush each one with melted butter, then lay 1½ tablespoons of the lobster filling at the end of each strip. Fold over the sides of the filo to cover the filling, then brush the edges with more melted butter and roll up; seal the edges with more melted butter. Repeat the process with the rest of the filling, making 8 rolls measuring about 3.5 x 8 cm (1½ x 3 inches). Lay the rolls on a greased baking sheet and bake in a preheated oven, 180°C (350°F), Gas Mark 4, for 20 minutes or until golden brown.

3. Meanwhile, make the wasabi and ginger sauce. Mix the sake or vermouth and soy sauce, then stir in the wasabi and ginger. Pour into tiny dishes. Serve the hot lobster rolls with the cool dipping sauce, placing one dish by each place.

herb and spice information: spring onions p10; garlic p11; ginger p89; wasabi p86

grilled prawns
with chilli oil

*Large freshwater king prawns, sold raw in the shell,
but with the heads removed are the best for grilling.
Tiger prawns are also good, so long as they too are
raw. Offer a green salad with the prawns.*

3 tablespoons virgin olive oil

½ teaspoon crushed chilli flakes

16–20 large raw prawns

2 limes, cut in quarters, to garnish

Serves 4
as a main dish.

1. Put the oil in a small pan with the chilli flakes.
Warm gently over low heat for 4 minutes, then leave
to cool.

2. When ready to cook, heat the grill and thread the
prawns on skewers, leaving their shells on. Allow
4–5 prawns for each person. Brush the prawns on
both sides with the chilli oil and grill for 3 minutes on
each side.

3. The prawns may be served on the skewers, or slid
off on to a mound of buttered rice mixed with
chopped herbs, if you like. Serve with quartered
limes and a bowl of mayonnaise.

Note: For a tidy dish, you may prefer to shell the
prawns before grilling. In this case grill for 2 minutes
on each side.

herb and spice information: chillies p56

1 dried Guajillo chilli

3 tablespoons olive oil

1 onion, thinly sliced

2 garlic cloves, finely chopped

250 g (8 oz) tomatoes, skinned and deseeded

2 strips lemon rind, finely chopped

6 tablespoons orange juice

10 scallops, cleaned

250 g (8 oz) squid, cleaned

500 g (1 lb) monkfish fillet, cut into 2.5 cm (1 inch) cubes

1 tablespoon lemon juice

3 tablespoons roughly chopped coriander leaves

salt and black pepper

Serves 4

My friend and colleague, Sybil Kapoor, has been kind enough to give me this recipe, which is, she says, an example of how to use one of the many varieties of dried chilli now available. Guajillo chillies have a distinctive mild, rich flavour, almost fruity, but most of the larger dried chillies may be used, except for the extra hot habañeros and Scotch bonnets. The fish and shellfish can be varied to taste.

1. Roast the chilli in a preheated oven, 160°C (325°F), Gas Mark 3, for 3–5 minutes or until it softens and releases a delicious aroma. (Never use burnt chillies, as they are very bitter.) Remove the stalk and seeds, and soak the roasted chilli for at least 20 minutes in 4 tablespoons of boiling water. Drain the chilli. reserving the water, and purée it in a small food mill with 2 tablespoons of its soaking water. Guajillo skins are very tough, so strain the purée before setting aside.

2. Heat the olive oil in a large saucepan and gently fry the onion and garlic until soft and golden. Add the chilli purée to the onions and evaporate all the liquid before adding the tomatoes. Season with salt and black pepper, simmer gently until the tomatoes disintegrate into a mush, then stir in the lemon rind and orange juice with 3–4 tablespoons water, using just enough to thin down the mixture slightly. Simmer for a further 20 minutes, adding a little more water if the mixture seems too thick. The flavours will develop subtly if the sauce is then cooled and refrigerated overnight.

3. Cut the cleaned scallops in half. Thoroughly rinse the cleaned squid and slice into thin rings or strips. When ready to serve, bring the sauce back to the boil and add the monkfish. Simmer gently for 4 minutes before adding the scallops. Cook for 3 minutes, until the scallops are white and just firm, before adding the squid and lemon juice. Allow to cook for a further 4 minutes, then check the seasoning. Add the chopped coriander leaves and serve with rice.

herb and spice information: chillies p56; garlic p11; coriander leaves p22

spicy seafood
stew

braised pheasant
with lovage

4 tablespoons olive oil

1 young pheasant, preferably a hen

1 small onion, sliced

2 leeks, sliced

2 carrots, sliced

1½ tablespoons chopped oregano
or marjoram

15 g (½ oz) lovage leaves

125 ml (4 fl oz) chicken stock

125 ml (4 fl oz) red wine

1 teaspoon plain flour

5 g (¼ oz) butter, at room
temperature

salt and black pepper

1½ tablespoons roughly chopped
flat-leaf parsley, to garnish

Serves 2 to 3

1. Heat the oil in a flameproof casserole and brown the bird, turning frequently. Remove the bird and put the sliced vegetables in the pan. Cook gently, stirring now and then, for 5 minutes, then spread them out in an even layer in the bottom of the pan and lay the bird on top. Sprinkle with the oregano or marjoram and tuck the lovage around the bird.

2. Heat the stock and wine together and pour over the bird. Add salt and pepper, cover and cook in a preheated oven, 160°C (325°F), Gas Mark 3, for about 1¼ hours. Allow an extra 5 minutes for a cock bird; longer still for old birds. Test to see when it is done by piercing a leg with a thin skewer; the juices should run faintly pink.

3. Meanwhile, stir the flour into the butter to make a smooth paste. Remove the bird from the casserole and keep warm. Discard the lovage leaves. Set the casserole over a low heat and drop in the flour-and-butter paste in small pieces, stirring constantly as each piece is added and until it is smoothly blended. Simmer for 3 minutes.

4. Joint or carve the pheasant. Lay the meat on a shallow dish and spoon the vegetables in their sauce over and around the bird. Scatter the chopped parsley over all and serve, with a purée of potatoes and a green vegetable.

Note: If you choose to braise two birds, to serve 4–6, the same amount of vegetables and other ingredients will suffice.

poussins with thyme and garlic

25 g (1 oz) butter

3 tablespoons sunflower oil

2 poussins

12 garlic cloves, unpeeled

150 ml (¼ pint) dry white wine

4 sprigs thyme

1 shallot, chopped

50 g (2 oz) chicken livers, cut in pieces

2 tablespoons crème fraîche or double cream

salt and black pepper

Garnish:

¼ tablespoon finely chopped parsley

75 g (3 oz) mâche

Serves 4

When made with squabs (farmed pigeons) instead of poussins, this is even more delicious, but much more expensive. Serve with boiled rice, noodles or new potatoes, and a salad.

1. Heat the butter in a flameproof casserole with 2 tablespoons of the oil. Add the birds and brown them all over. Take out the birds and put the garlic cloves into the casserole. Cook very gently for 1–2 minutes, then add the wine, thyme and salt and pepper. Bring to the boil, lay the birds on the garlic and cover the casserole. Cook in a preheated oven, 190°C (375°F), Gas Mark 5, for 30–35 minutes.

2. Meanwhile, heat the remaining oil in a frying pan. Add the chopped shallot and cook gently for 1–2 minutes. Then add the chicken livers and continue to cook briefly, until they are just cooked through. Set aside.

3. Transfer the poussins to a plate and keep warm. Discard the thyme and push the garlic cloves through a medium food mill into a bowl. Purée the livers and shallots and pour on to the garlic. Put the casserole over a low heat and add the purée to the juices, stirring to blend well. Add the crème fraîche or double cream and salt and pepper to taste. Heat gently, then pour into a bowl and sprinkle with chopped parsley.

4. Make a bed of mâche on a flat dish. Cut the birds in half and lay them on it. Serve the sauce separately.

herb and spice information: garlic p11; thyme p47; parsley p36

poached chicken
in herb sauce

4 boneless chicken breasts, skinned

2 large spring onions, sliced

2 x 5 mm (¼ inch) slices fresh root ginger

10 black peppercorns, lightly crushed

½ teaspoon sea salt

Herb Sauce:

25 g (1 oz) butter

1½ tablespoons plain flour

150 ml (¼ pint) single cream

½ tablespoon chopped chervil

½ tablespoon chopped dill

½ tablespoon chopped tarragon

salt and black pepper

Serves 4

Offer rice, noodles or new potatoes, and a green salad with this simple, yet delicious, chicken dish.

1. Put the chicken breasts into a saucepan and add enough water to cover them. Remove the chicken and put the spring onions, ginger, peppercorns and salt into the pan. Bring to the boil, replace the chicken breasts, bring back to the boil, and simmer gently for 10 minutes, or until the chicken breasts are cooked through.

2. Lift out the chicken breasts and strain the stock. Measure 300 ml (½ pint) of the stock and set it aside. Put the chicken back in the remaining stock to keep warm while you make the sauce.

3. To make the sauce, melt the butter, add the flour and cook for 1 minute, stirring. Then add the 300 ml (½ pint) chicken stock and bring to the boil, stirring. Simmer gently for 3 minutes, stirring from time to time. Add the cream and salt and pepper to taste. Finally, stir in the chopped herbs and remove from the heat.

4. To serve, lay the chicken breasts on a flat dish and pour some of the sauce over them. Serve the rest separately in a small jug.

herb and spice information: spring onions p10; ginger p89; pepper p79; chervil p15; dill p13; tarragon p17

green curried
chicken

500 g (1 lb) boneless chicken
breasts, skinned and cut in strips
or cubes

250 g (8 oz) onions, sliced

4 tablespoons sunflower oil

2 tablespoons Green Curry Paste
(see page 189)

450 ml (¾ pint) chicken stock,
heated

300 ml (½ pint) coconut milk

3 tablespoons tamarind water (see
page 84) or semi-acidic fruit juice,
such as Seville orange, pink
grapefruit, or lime

salt and black pepper

15 fresh curry leaves (optional)

Marinade:

1 teaspoon sea salt

20 black peppercorns

2 large garlic cloves, crushed

50 g (2 oz) fresh root ginger, peeled
and crushed or finely chopped

Serves 4

Neither tamarind nor curry leaves are essential for this dish, but coconut milk definitely is.

1. To make the marinade, put the sea salt and black peppercorns in a mortar and pound briefly. Add the crushed garlic and ginger and pound again, just until amalgamated. Transfer to a dish just large enough to hold the chicken. Turn the chicken pieces in the marinade and mix well. Set aside for a few hours or overnight.

2. Cook the sliced onions slowly in the oil, allowing about 12 minutes for them to soften and colour. Then add the curry paste and cook gently for 8 minutes, stirring often. Now add the chicken pieces, stirring until they have browned all over.

3. Pour in the heated stock, add salt and black pepper, and simmer for 20 minutes. Then add the coconut milk, tamarind water or fruit juice and the curry leaves, if using. Cook for another 3 minutes. Turn into a dish and serve with basmati rice.

herb and spice information: tamarind p84; curry leaves p21; pepper p79; garlic p11; ginger p89

stir-fried chicken
with red pepper flakes

2 boneless chicken breasts, cut into
thin strips

4 tablespoons soy sauce

½ teaspoon sugar (optional)

5 cm (2 inch) piece fresh root ginger,
peeled and cut in 1 cm
(½ inch) chunks

3–4 tablespoons sunflower oil

2 onions, sliced

3 garlic cloves, sliced

½ teaspoon crushed chilli flakes

200 g (7 oz) bean sprouts, rinsed

3 tablespoons chopped coriander
leaves, to garnish

Serves 4

1. Put the chicken strips in a bowl. Pour the soy sauce over them and add the sugar, if using. Crush the ginger in a garlic press and add the juice to the chicken strips; discard the debris left in the press. Let the chicken stand for 30 minutes.

2. Heat a wok. Add enough oil to cover the bottom and heat again, then throw in the sliced onion and garlic. Cook for 3–4 minutes, stirring, then add the chicken and its marinade, and the red pepper flakes. Stir-fry for 4 minutes or until the chicken is cooked through. Add the bean sprouts and cook for 1 minute longer. Turn on to a dish and scatter with the chopped coriander.

Note: Rump steak or pork fillet may be used instead of the chicken.

herb and spice information: ginger p89; garlic p11; chillies p56; coriander leaves p22

750 g (1½ lb) celeriac, quartered and thinly sliced

3 tablespoons sunflower oil

300 ml (½ pint) chicken stock, heated

1 brace pheasants (1 cock, 1 hen)

6 stalks lemon grass

6 garlic cloves, unpeeled and roughly crushed

25 g (1 oz) fresh root ginger, cut in 4 and roughly crushed

6 juniper berries, roughly crushed

6 black peppercorns, roughly crushed

sea salt and black pepper

125 g (4 oz) mâche

1 Granny Smith apple, or other hard, green apple, peeled, quartered and thickly sliced

1½ tablespoons chopped chervil

Dressing:

2 tablespoons extra virgin olive oil

2 tablespoons lemon juice

1 tablespoon soy sauce or balsamic vinegar

Serves 6 to 8

braised pheasants with lemon grass

1. Start 1 day in advance. Heat 2 tablespoons sunflower oil in a large flameproof casserole. Add the celeriac and turn the slices in the oil for 6 minutes. Add the stock and salt and pepper, then bring to the boil. Reduce the heat, cover and cook gently for 45 minutes. Drain the celeriac, reserving the stock. Cover, cool and chill the celeriac.

2. Heat the remaining oil in the rinsed-out casserole and brown the birds all over. Sprinkle with salt and black pepper. Lay them on their sides and add the lemon grass, garlic, ginger, juniper berries and peppercorns. Pour in the reserved stock and bring to the boil. Cover and cook in a preheated oven, 190°C (375°F), Gas Mark 5, for 30 minutes. Remove the hen but cook the cock for another 5 minutes. Return the hen to the pan and leave to cool.

3. Next day, skim off the fat, remove the birds. Strain and reserve the stock. Remove and carve the breast meat from the birds, setting aside the remainder for another dish.

4. Prepare the dressing. Mix the oil and lemon juice with 2 tablespoons of the strained stock, then mix in the soy sauce or balsamic vinegar. Lay the mâche on a platter. Pour half the dressing over the mâche. Add the apple and celeriac.

5. Lay the pheasant on the salad and spoon over the rest of the dressing. Sprinkle with chervil and serve.

Note: The pheasants can be served hot. Allow an extra 5 minutes roasting, then carve as above, laying both joints and slices on a dish of cooked noodles. Omit the dressed salad base, but mix the strained and degreased pan juices with the soy sauce or balsamic vinegar, then pour over all.

herb and spice information: lemon grass p23; garlic p11; ginger p89; juniper berries p70;

pepper p79; chervil p15

133

pork sausages
with fresh herbs

300 g (10 oz) lean, boneless pork, from the leg

300 g (10 oz) belly of pork

75 g (3 oz) soft white breadcrumbs (use coarse country bread)

6 tablespoons milk

2 garlic cloves, chopped

2 teaspoons sea salt

1 teaspoon black peppercorns

12 juniper berries

¼ teaspoon ground mace

¼ teaspoon ground allspice

2 tablespoons coarsely chopped flat-leaf parsley

2 tablespoons coarsely chopped basil

Makes about 750 g (1½ lb).

Anyone with a sausage-making attachment for their mixer and a friendly butcher who will supply the skins, may like to try making sausages. Natural casings are made from the small intestines of the pig or sheep; synthetic skins are also available. Your butcher may even be prepared to fill sausage skins with your own filling. But do not consider making your own sausages without a food processor. The seasonings can be adjusted to your taste, but the use of fresh herbs (as opposed to the musty aroma of dried sage) can only be welcome.

1. Cut the leg of pork in cubes and put in the food processor. Separate the lean from the fat of the belly meat and add it, also cut in cubes, to the pork in the processor. Process both together until coarse in texture. Cut the fat from the belly into neat cubes about 5 mm (¼ inch). Mix all the meat together in a large bowl.

2. Soak the bread in the milk for 10 minutes, then squeeze it dry and add to the meat, mixing thoroughly. Crush the garlic in a mortar with the sea salt, peppercorns and juniper berries until most of the peppercorns are just broken, then stir into the meat with the ground spices. Lastly, stir in the chopped fresh herbs. Taste by frying a small ball in a drop of oil, and then adjust the seasonings to your liking.

3. Fill the sausage casings according to the directions that came with your machine, or ask your butcher to fill them. These sausages are best cooked slowly: either fried or grilled, or in a preheated oven, 180°C (350°F), Gas Mark 4, for 30–35 minutes.

Note: Instead of filling sausage casings, you could shape the sausagemeat into small round patties on a lightly floured surface. Cook the patties in the same way as sausages.

herb and spice information: garlic p11; pepper p79; juniper berries p70; mace p72; allspice p76; parsley p36; basil p33

Moroccan lamb
tagine

750 g (1½ lb) boneless lamb (½ a boned leg or shoulder), cubed

seasoned plain flour

3 tablespoons olive oil

2 onions, sliced

2 green peppers, cored, deseeded and cut in strips

1 head fennel, sliced

1 teaspoon ground ginger

½ teaspoon saffron threads

600 ml (1 pint) chicken or veal stock

125 g (4 oz) dried apricots, chopped

1–2 tablespoons lemon juice

sea salt and black pepper

Serves 4

A grain dish, such as couscous or basmati rice, or a wild rice, and a green salad are ideal accompaniments for this succulent spicy lamb.

1. Toss the lamb in seasoned flour. Heat the olive oil in a flameproof casserole and brown the lamb, stirring often. Using a slotted spoon, transfer the lamb to a plate. Add the sliced vegetables to the fat remaining in the casserole and cook gently for 4–5 minutes, stirring often, until they are lightly coloured. Stir in the ginger towards the end of the time. Replace the lamb.

2. Warm the saffron in a large metal spoon, over a gentle heat for about 30 seconds, then pound it in a mortar. Heat the stock and then add 2 tablespoons to the saffron; leave to infuse for a few minutes while you add the rest of the stock to the lamb with salt and black pepper to taste. Add the saffron infusion, cover the pan and simmer for 1 hour.

3. Finally, add the chopped apricots – they do not need soaking – and cook for a further 15 minutes. Adjust the seasoning, adding lemon juice to taste, and serve.

herb and spice information: ginger p89; saffron p61

braised breast of lamb with celery leaves

1 breast of lamb, boned

40 g (1½ oz) butter

2 onions, sliced

2 leeks, sliced

2 carrots, sliced

2 celery sticks, sliced

1 bay leaf

125 ml (4 fl oz) chicken stock

125 ml (4 fl oz) dry white wine

2 tablespoons flat-leaf parsley, torn in bits, to garnish

Stuffing:

50 g (2 oz) dry white bread, crusts removed

125 ml (4 fl oz) milk

250 g (8 oz) spinach

2 tablespoons roughly chopped celery leaves or lovage

¼ teaspoon mace

1 egg yolk

salt and black pepper

Serves 3 to 4

1. First make the stuffing. Soak the bread in the milk for 10 minutes, then squeeze dry. Drop the spinach into lightly salted boiling water and cook briskly for 4–5 minutes, depending on the time of year. (Tender summer spinach needs only 4 minutes.) Drain in a colander, rinse under cold running water and drain again. Leave until cool enough to handle, then squeeze out the excess moisture and chop coarsely. Mix with the bread, adding the chopped celery leaves or lovage, mace, egg yolk and salt and pepper to taste. Mix well.

2. Lay out the breast of lamb and spread the stuffing evenly over it, leaving 5 mm (¼ inch) clear around the edges. Roll up firmly and tie securely around the middle with 3–4 pieces of string.

3. Heat the butter in a flameproof casserole, add the sliced vegetables and stew them gently for 5 minutes, stirring occasionally. Remove most of the vegetables with a slotted spoon. Add the lamb and brown gently all over, turning often. Pack the vegetables back around the meat and add the bay leaf. Heat the stock and wine together and pour over the meat. Bring to the boil, then cover and cook in a preheated oven, 150°C (300°F), Gas Mark 2, for 2 hours.

4. Lift out the meat and carve in thick slices. Using a slotted spoon, transfer the sliced vegetables to a serving dish. Discard the bay leaf. Lay the sliced meat over the vegetables and keep warm. Strain the stock and skim off excess fat. Use a few spoonfuls of the stock to moisten the meat, and serve the separately. Garnish with parsley and serve with a purée of potatoes and a green salad.

herb and spice information: bay leaves p27; parsley p36; celery leaves p16; lovage p29; mace p72

1 teaspoon ground coriander

½ tablespoon ground cumin

½ teaspoon Harissa (see page 186)

2 tablespoons tomato purée

1.5 kg (3 lb) neck of lamb, unboned and cut in large pieces

75 ml (3 fl oz) olive oil

125 g (4 oz) pickling onions, peeled

175 g (6 oz) thin leeks, cut in chunks

175 g (6 oz) small carrots, sliced

175 g (6 oz) small turnips, quartered

250 g (8 oz) courgettes, chopped

175 g (6 oz) tomatoes, skinned and quartered

125 g (4 oz) shelled peas

sea salt and black pepper

500 g (1 lb) couscous

Garnish:

½ teaspoon saffron threads

125 g (4 oz) canned chickpeas, heated

2 tablespoons torn coriander leaves (optional)

Hot Sauce I or II (see page 188)

This is not nearly as much trouble to make as it looks, and it is truly a wonderful dish.

1. Mix the ground coriander, cumin, harissa, sea salt and black pepper into the tomato purée, then rub the resulting paste all over the pieces of lamb. Leave for 1–2 hours.

2. Next prepare the couscous, put it in a bowl and pour 600 ml (1 pint) cold water over it. Leave for 10 minutes, then stir with a spoon, breaking up any lumps, and sprinkle 2 teaspoons of the olive oil over it. Tip the couscous into the top of a couscousier; if you don't have one, line a metal colander or large strainer with muslin and tip the couscous into it.

3. In the bottom of the couscousier or in a large pan over which the strainer fits, heat the remaining olive oil and brown the pieces of lamb slowly, allowing about 10 minutes. Pour in enough hot water to cover the lamb and bring to the boil. Boil for 30 minutes, then add the onions, leeks, carrots and turnips, adding more boiling water to come level with the vegetables. Add salt and pepper to taste. Stand the couscous over the lamb and cover with a lid or foil. Bring back to the boil and cook steadily for a further 30 minutes. Add the courgettes and cook for 15 minutes. Add the tomatoes and the peas and cook for a final 15 minutes. By now the lamb should have been cooking for 1½ hours and the couscous for 1 hour; both should be ready at the same time.

4. To serve, toast the saffron threads in a large metal spoon over a gentle heat, shaking them to and fro for about 30 seconds. Then pound them in a mortar. Tip the couscous on to a large platter, breaking up any lumps. Lift the vegetables out of the sauce with a slotted spoon and lay them on the couscous. Scatter the chickpeas and torn coriander leaves, if using, over the top. Lay the lamb on a separate dish. Add 2 tablespoons of the lamb sauce to the saffron. Pound a few times, to mix, then tip back into the sauce. Serve the sauce separately, with a small dish of Hot Sauce I or II also on the table.

herb and spice information: coriander seeds (ground) p60; cumin seeds (ground) p62; saffron p61

lamb couscous

coriander steak

2 tablespoons coriander seeds

1 tablespoon black mustard seeds

2 teaspoons black peppercorns

2 teaspoons sea salt

4 sirloin steaks

25 g (1 oz) butter

1½ tablespoons sunflower oil

Serves 4

This recipe is an aromatic version of steak au poivre, based on whole coriander seeds instead of peppercorns.

1. Put the coriander seeds in a mortar with the mustard seeds, peppercorns and sea salt. Crush them roughly, then use to coat the steaks on both sides. Leave for 1 hour or longer.

2. Heat the butter and oil in a heavy frying pan. When the fat is very hot, put in the steaks and fry briefly on each side. Try to keep the spices on the meat. Serve with a Smoky Salsa (see page 190), served at room temperature.

herb and spice information: coriander seeds p60; mustard seeds p83; pepper p79

Gnocchi can be made successfully only with floury old potatoes, and these can be found only during the winter months. Large 'new' potatoes, which are sold as 'suitable for mashing' during the summer months, just will not do.

1. Boil the potatoes in their skins, then drain well. Once they are cool enough to handle, peel them, and push through a medium food mill into the same pan. Dry out by stirring for a few moments over gentle heat, then turn into a bowl. Beat in the sifted flour, butter, egg yolk and salt and pepper to taste. Turn out the dough on to a floured surface and knead lightly once or twice, then cut in quarters. Form each quarter into a roll about 2.5 cm (1 inch) thick. Rest the dough while you make the pesto.

750 g (1½ lb) floury old potatoes

125 g (4 oz) plain flour, sifted

25 g (1 oz) butter, cut into small pieces

1 egg yolk, beaten

Rocket Pesto (see page 184)

salt and black pepper

Garnish:

15 g (½ oz) butter (optional)

50 g (2 oz) freshly grated Parmesan cheese

Serves 4 as a first course, or 3 to 4 as a light main dish.

2. Shortly before serving, bring a wide pan of lightly salted water to the boil. Cut the rolls of potato dough into slices about 1 cm (½ inch) thick, and press each one gently into the palm of your hand, using the prongs of a fork to give a lightly ridged effect. When all are done, drop them, a few at a time, into the gently simmering water. Cook for about 3 minutes after the water comes back to the boil. Shortly after the gnocchi rise to the surface, lift them out with a slotted spoon. Transfer to a colander and drain briefly, while you cook the second lot. Then transfer the first batch to a heated serving dish and keep warm.

3. When all are done, add just enough pesto to give a generous coating – don't drown them – folding it in lightly. Dot with butter, if using, and sprinkle with a little freshly grated Parmesan. Serve immediately, with the remaining Parmesan in a small bowl.

Note: There will be quite a lot of pesto left over; it can be frozen or refrigerated for serving with other pasta dishes.

herb and spice information: rocket p24

potato gnocchi
with rocket pesto

potato & lentil patties with cucumber and yogurt sauce

250 g (8 oz) freshly mashed potato

375 g (12 oz) cooked green lentils

3 tablespoons sunflower oil

½ bunch spring onions, chopped

1–2 green chillies, deseeded and finely chopped

1 teaspoon ground cumin

1 teaspoon ground coriander

2 tablespoons chopped mint

1 egg, beaten

a little plain flour, sifted

25 g (1 oz) butter

salt and black pepper

Cucumber and Yogurt Sauce (see page 180)

Serves 4

1. Put the mashed potato in a large bowl and stand a coarse food mill over it. Push the cooked lentils through the mill and mix well with the potato, beating with a wooden spoon.

2. Heat 2 tablespoons of the sunflower oil in a frying pan and cook the chopped spring onions, adding the chillies after 1–2 minutes. Then add the cumin and coriander and cook gently for 2–3 minutes, stirring constantly. Tip the contents of the frying pan on to the potato–lentil purée and mix well, adding plenty of salt and pepper. Stir in the chopped mint.

3. Form the mixture into 8 round patties on a lightly floured surface. Place on a floured plate, cover and chill for several hours or overnight.

4. To cook the patties. Heat the butter with the remaining oil in a large frying pan. Dip the patties in beaten egg and coat in flour, then add to the hot fat. you will probably have to cook the patties in two batches (unless you have a very large frying pan). Cook them quite quickly, turning once, until browned on both sides and well heated through. Drain on kitchen paper, then keep warm while you fry the second batch. Serve as soon as possible, with the chilled cucumber and yogurt sauce in a separate bowl.

herb and spice information: spring onions p10; chillies p56; cumin seeds (ground) p62; coriander seeds (ground) p60; mint p31

steamed rice in a bowl with herbs

250 g (8 oz) brown basmati rice

6 tablespoons sunflower oil

1 bunch spring onions, sliced

6 tablespoons chopped mixed herbs, such as flat-leaf parsley, tarragon, oregano, chervil

a few dashes of light soy sauce

Serves 4

1. Put the rice in a saucepan, add 600 ml (1 pint) lightly salted water and bring to the boil. Lower the heat as much as possible, cover the pan and cook for 20 minutes or until the water has been absorbed. Meanwhile, grease 4 small 300 ml (½ pint) bowls with oil.

2. Heat 4 tablespoons of the oil gently and cook the sliced spring onions for 2–3 minutes. Then throw in the chopped herbs and stir around for 1 minute over a low heat, just long enough to warm and soften the herbs. Divide the spring onion and herb mixture between the prepared bowls and sprinkle with a little light soy sauce. Pile the brown rice on to the herbs, adding a drizzle of oil and a dash of soy as you do so. Cover each little bowl with a piece of foil.

3. If serving immediately, simply stand the bowls in a steamer, covered, over boiling water for about 8 minutes. Alternatively, they may be kept for up to 1 week in the refrigerator, and brought to room temperature, then steamed for 15 minutes before serving. To serve, turn them out on to flat plates and accompany with 2–3 simply cooked vegetables.

Note: Other grains may be used instead of brown basmati rice: white basmati rice; a mixture of wild and brown or white rice; buckwheat; or couscous. Simply cook the grain according to the packet instructions, then proceed as above. If you don't have any small bowls, one large bowl holding about 1.2 litres (2 pints) may be used instead. In this case, steam it for 20 minutes if freshly made or 45 minutes if reheating from room temperature.

green risotto

2 shallots, finely chopped

3 tablespoons olive oil

1 garlic clove, finely chopped

250 g (8 oz) risotto rice, washed and drained

750 ml (1¼ pints) chicken stock, heated

1½ tablespoons chopped robust herbs, such as lovage, oregano, thyme

a pinch of saffron threads

1½ tablespoons chopped tender herbs, such as dill, chervil, tarragon

40 g (1½ oz) freshly grated Parmesan cheese

Serves 3 to 4

1. Cook the chopped shallots slowly in the oil for 3 minutes, then add the garlic and cook for another minute. Put the rice in the pan, stir around in the oil for 1 minute, then add half the heated stock and the robust herbs. Simmer the rice slowly in the stock, stirring often, for about 8 minutes, or until the stock has almost all been absorbed.

2. Meanwhile, pour 2–3 tablespoonfuls of the remaining hot stock over the saffron in a small bowl and set aside. Add the saffron liquid and half the remaining stock to the rice. When that also has been absorbed, the rice will probably be tender. If not, add the rest of the stock and cook a few minutes longer.

3. Shortly before serving, stir in the tender herbs, turn on to a serving dish, and sprinkle with the grated Parmesan. The risotto must be served immediately or the grains of rice will stick together.

herb and spice information: garlic p11; lovage p29; oregano p35; thyme p47; saffron p61; dill p13; chervil p15; tarragon p17

pasta with aubergine, peppers and chillies

This is a beautiful dish, with glowing, jewel-like colours.

1. Sprinkle the aubergine slices on both sides with salt and leave for 30 minutes. Soak the chillies for 20 minutes in 4 tablespoons boiling water. Drain the chillies, reserving the water and purée them with half their soaking water.

2. Rinse the salt off the aubergine slices. Pat dry and brush with a little of the olive oil. Grill them, or cook on a ridged cast-iron grill pan on top of the heat, until browned, then cut across in diagonal strips about 2.5 cm (1 inch) wide. Cut the onion half into 2 wedges. Then cut each wedge across to make 4 chunky pieces. Separate the pieces into individual layers.

1 aubergine, cut in 1 cm (½ inch) thick slices

2 dried chillies, deseeded and stalks removed

4–6 tablespoons olive oil

½ large Spanish onion

6 large garlic cloves, peeled

1 red pepper, grilled, skinned and deseeded

1 yellow pepper, grilled, skinned and deseeded

400 g (13 oz) fresh fettucine or other flat noodles

3 tablespoons flat-leaf parsley, chopped

sea salt and black pepper

Serves 4

3. Heat 3 tablespoons olive oil in a heavy pan and add the onion pieces. Cook gently for 5 minutes, then add the whole garlic cloves and continue to cook gently for another 10 minutes, until the onion has softened, but not browned.

4. Cut the skinned peppers across in broad diagonal strips, like the aubergines, and add to the onions with the chilli purée. Add sea salt and black pepper, and cook for 5 minutes. Then add the strips of grilled aubergine and reheat the vegetables gently together for 4–5 minutes.

5. Meanwhile, cook the pasta in lightly salted boiling water for 4–5 minutes, or until tender, then drain. Add the chopped parsley to the vegetable mixture and serve over the pasta.

potato cakes
with cumin

A fresh tomato sauce, tomato salad or salsa of fresh tomatoes goes well with these potato cakes.

1. Boil, thoroughly drain and peel the potatoes. Push them through a medium food mill and return to a clean pan. Dry out over gentle heat, then set aside.

2. Heat half the oil in a frying pan and cook the spring onions for 3 minutes, adding the cumin half way through. Tip on to the potato purée and mix well, adding the chopped coriander leaves, and sea salt and black pepper to taste. Chill the mixture for 1 hour until firm, if possible.

3. Divide the mixture into 8 equal portions and form into small round cakes, shaping them on a floured board. Mix the turmeric, saffron or curry powder with the breadcrumbs or sifted flour. Dip the cakes first in the beaten egg, then in the breadcrumbs or flour.

4. Heat the remaining oil in a frying pan and cook the cakes until golden on each side, about 6 minutes in all. Drain them briefly on kitchen paper, then serve.

Note: If rushed, simply coat the cakes in flour and omit the egg and breadcrumbs.

750 g (1½ lb) floury potatoes

3 tablespoons sunflower oil

1 bunch spring onions, sliced

2 teaspoons ground cumin

2 tablespoons chopped coriander leaves

1 teaspoon ground turmeric, powdered saffron or mild curry powder

8 tablespoons dry white breadcrumbs or sifted plain flour

1 egg, beaten

sea salt and black pepper

Makes 8; serves 4

herb and spice information: spring onions p10; cumin seeds (ground) p62; coriander leaves p22; turmeric p63; saffron p61

mushrooms
stuffed with aubergine and peppers

1 large aubergine

8 medium to large flat mushrooms

3 tablespoons sunflower oil

2 yellow peppers

6 large spring onions, sliced

3 tablespoons extra virgin olive oil

1½ tablespoons lemon juice

3 tablespoons roughly chopped flat-leaf parsley

salt and black pepper

Serves 4 as a first course

1. Bake the aubergine in a preheated oven, 180°C (350°F), Gas Mark 4, for 1 hour, turning often. Set aside to cool. Lay the mushrooms, gills up, on an oiled baking sheet. Brush the gills with sunflower oil, allowing about 1 teaspoon of oil for each mushroom. Bake the the mushrooms in the oven for the final 15 minutes. They should be just softened; do not allow them to collapse. Take the aubergine and mushrooms out of the oven and leave to cool.

2. Cut the peppers in half, discard the stalks and seeds, and grill until the skin has blackened and blistered all over. Set them aside to cool.

3. Cut the aubergine in half and scoop out the inside. Chop the flesh roughly by hand, then mash it with a fork. Do not be tempted to put it in a food processor, as it should not be too smooth. Peel or scrape the skin off the grilled peppers and cut the flesh into neat dice. Stir the diced pepper into the aubergine purée, then add the sliced spring onions. Finally, stir in the olive oil and lemon juice, parsley, and salt and pepper to taste.

4. Mound the aubergine stuffing on the mushrooms and place on a flat dish. Serve at room temperature.

herb and spice information: spring onions p10; parsley p36

braised celery
with lovage

3 heads celery, trimmed and halved

50 g (2 oz) butter

600 ml (1 pint) game, chicken or
vegetable stock

1 tablespoon lemon juice

1½ tablespoons chopped lovage

salt and black pepper

Sauce (optional):

1 teaspoon plain flour

15 g (½ oz) butter, at room
temperature

75 ml (3 fl oz) soured cream

Serves 4

1. Blanch the halved celery for 5 minutes in fast boiling water, then drain in a colander. Rub a heavy flameproof casserole with some of the butter and lay the celery in it, in one layer if possible. Dot with the rest of the butter. Heat the stock and pour half of it over the celery, adding the lemon juice, chopped lovage, and salt and pepper.

2. Cover and cook gently over a very low heat for 1½–2 hours, until the celery is tender all the way through. Turn the pieces over every 30 minutes, adding more stock as required. Start testing the celery with a skewer after 1½ hours: when the pieces are ready, transfer them to a serving dish and pour the juices over them. Alternatively, the juices can be made into a sauce in the following way.

3. Stir the flour into the butter to make a smooth paste. Drop small pieces of this into the cooking juices in the casserole, stirring vigorously until each piece is mixed in and the sauce is free from lumps. Bring to the boil, then cook gently for 3 minutes, then add the soured cream, and salt and pepper to taste. Finally, pour the cream sauce over the celery.

Note: I like this best with the juices left unthickened when serving with game, poultry and beef, but I like the cream sauce for serving with other vegetable dishes or a bowl of brown rice. Lovage is hard to find in shops, but easily grown in the garden. Failing all else, use celery leaves instead.

herb and spice information: lovage p29

comfrey fritters

Comfrey is one of those herbs with large hairy leaves which make excellent fritters. This batter, made with soda water or sparkling mineral water, is eminently suited to delicate foods like leaves.

1. A batter made with sparkling water should not be allowed to stand, so prepare it just before use. Prepare the comfrey leaves first: trim off the stalks, rinse the leaves carefully under cold running water, then shake and pat dry in a cloth.

2. Shortly before serving, heat a large pan of clean vegetable oil until hot enough to brown a small cube of bread in 20 seconds (180°C/350°F). While the oil is heating, make the batter. Sift the flour with the salt into a food processor or large bowl. Add the oil, processing or beating by hand, then start to add the sparkling water gradually, processing or beating constantly, stopping when the batter has reached the consistency of fairly thick cream. Whisk the egg white until stiff and fold it into the batter.

3. Dip each leaf in the batter, scraping off the excess on the sides of the bowl, then drop it into the hot oil. Cook a few leaves at a time for about 3 minutes, then lift them out and drain on kitchen paper while you cook the next batch. As soon as the leaves have drained, transfer them to a warm dish. Garnish with lemon quarters and serve alone or with other dishes.

comfrey leaves

vegetable oil for frying

lemon quarters, to garnish

Batter:

125 g (4 oz) plain flour

a pinch of salt

2 tablespoons sunflower oil

150 ml (1¼ pint) soda water or sparkling mineral water

1 egg white

grilled
vegetables
with basil

1 large red pepper, halved and deseeded

1 large yellow pepper

1 aubergine

4–6 tablespoons olive oil

2 courgettes

3 small leeks

2 heads fennel

3 small red onions

Dressing:

1 large garlic clove, finely chopped

2 heaped tablespoons basil, torn in bits

4 tablespoons extra virgin olive oil

½ tablespoon white wine vinegar

sea salt and black pepper

Serves 4 to 6 as a first course

This appetizing dish may be prepared several hours beforehand, but be sure to serve it at room temperature, not chilled. Offer crusty bread to mop up the delicious dressing.

1. Stick each pepper firmly on a long skewer. Heat the grill and put the peppers under it, turning them at regular intervals, until the skins are blackened all over. Remove and set aside to cool.

2. Cut a thin slice off each side of the aubergine and discard. Cut the rest of the aubergine lengthways in slices 1 cm (½ inch) thick. Brush them on both sides with a little of the olive oil, then place under the grill and cook until nicely coloured and softened, turning once. Set aside to cool.

3. Cut the courgettes in diagonal slices about the same thickness as the aubergine. Brush with olive oil on both sides and grill until speckled golden brown and fairly soft. Set aside to cool.

4. Trim the leeks down to the white parts. If very small, leave them whole, otherwise split them in half lengthways. Drop them into lightly salted boiling water and cook for 5 minutes, then drain well and pat dry in a cloth. Brush with olive oil and grill until lightly coloured.

5. Cut the fennel lengthways into slices about 1 cm (½ inch) thick. Brush with olive oil and grill until coloured, turning once. Then set aside.

6. Cut the red onions into fairly thick horizontal slices, allowing 4 slices to each onion. Brush them with olive oil and grill until they are soft and slightly blackened.

7. Arrange the vegetables on a flat dish. Sprinkle with garlic, basil, salt and pepper. Mix the oil and vinegar together and pour it over all.

herb and spice information: garlic p11; basil p33

saffron vegetable stew

4 small carrots, cut in 1 cm (½ inch) chunks

4 tablespoons olive oil

3 small leeks, cut in 1 cm (½ inch) slices

1 head fennel, halved and thinly sliced

3 courgettes, cut in 1 cm (½ inch) slices

2 bunches large spring onions, trimmed

2 tomatoes, skinned and cut in quarters

¼ teaspoon saffron threads

300 ml (½ pint) chicken or vegetable stock, heated

salt and black pepper

Serves 4

1. Drop the carrots into lightly salted boiling water and cook for 3 minutes, then drain. Heat the oil in a heavy pan and drop in the sliced leeks, carrots and sliced fennel. Cook gently for 4 minutes, then add the sliced courgettes and cook for another 4 minutes. Add the whole spring onions and quartered tomatoes, and then cook for another 2–3 minutes.

2. Steep the saffron in 3 tablespoons of the hot stock for 5 minutes, then add to the pan with the rest of the stock, salt and black pepper. Bring to the boil, cover the pan and simmer gently for 30 minutes. Serve hot, with couscous or basmati rice.

carrots and courgettes
with sesame

2½ tablespoons sunflower oil

250 g (8 oz) carrots, cut in thin
diagonal slices

250 g (8 oz) courgettes, cut in thin
diagonal slices

dash sesame oil

1½ tablespoons sesame seeds,
lightly toasted

sea salt and black pepper

Serves 2 to 3

Sesame-flavoured dishes like this one go well with roast and grilled poultry and other vegetables. I like to eat this dish with brown rice and a dash of Maggi Liquid Seasoning.

1. Heat the oil in a wok or large frying pan and throw in the carrots. Toss for 3 minutes, then add the courgettes and continue to toss for another 3 minutes, adding sea salt and black pepper.

2. Add a dash of sesame oil – not too much, for it is very strong – and stir in the toasted sesame seeds.

Variation: Instead of slicing the vegetables, use a swivel-blade vegetable peeler to cut them downwards in long, thin ribbons. Use 125 g (4 oz) each of carrots and courgettes, and 2 tablespoons oil. Cook the carrots for 4 minutes and the courgettes for 2 minutes.

herb and spice information: sesame seeds p82

green salad with herbs and flowers

2 Little Gem lettuces

10 sorrel leaves, cut in thin strips

10 sprigs chervil

5 marigolds, petals only, or 10 nasturtiums

Dressing:

1 tablespoon lemon juice

1 tablespoon white wine vinegar

4 tablespoons light olive oil

a pinch of sugar

a pinch of mustard powder

sea salt and black pepper

Serves 4

1. Separate the lettuces into leaves, wash them and drain well. Pile them in a bowl and lay the sorrel and chervil over them.

2. Mix together all the ingredients for the dressing and pour it over the salad, then toss well. Scatter the marigold petals or the whole nasturtiums on top and serve.

herb and spice information: sorrel p41; chervil p15; marigolds p20; nasturtiums p48; mustard seeds (powder) p83

rocket and watermelon salad with feta cheese and mint

75 g (3 oz) rocket, stalks removed

200 g (7 oz) watermelon, cubed

125 g (4 oz) feta cheese, cubed

24 large mint leaves, cut in strips, to garnish

Dressing:

1 tablespoon orange juice

1 tablespoon lemon juice

1 tablespoon white wine vinegar

3 tablespoons extra virgin olive oil

¼ teaspoon sugar

¼ teaspoon Dijon mustard

salt and black pepper

Serves 4 as a first course.

1 Wash the rocket and pat it dry in a cloth. Lay the leaves in a bowl. Arrange the cubed watermelon and feta cheese over the rocket.

2 Mix all the dressing ingredients together and pour over the salad. Toss well or leave most of the watermelon and feta on top, then toss the salad at the table, just before it is served. Sprinkle the strips of mint over all the salad. Serve immediately.

2 kg (4 lb) roasting chicken

1 onion, quartered

1 leek, quartered

1 large carrot, quartered

1 celery stick, halved

1 bay leaf

½ tablespoon sea salt

10 black peppercorns

Salad:

6 sun-dried tomato pieces, rinsed

125 g (4 oz) rocket, mâche or young spinach leaves, washed and drained

¼ cucumber, peeled, quartered lengthways and sliced

1 red chilli, deseeded and cut in thin rings

Dressing:

5 tablespoons extra virgin olive oil

2 tablespoons lemon juice

½ tablespoon white wine vinegar

5–6 drops chilli oil

Serves 4

A large poached chicken will provide enough white meat for the salad and produce a well-flavoured stock for making fabulous soup. This dish deserves an organically reared, or at least free-range, bird for optimum flavour and texture. Serve it with a few slices of toasted pitta bread.

1. Begin 1 day in advance. Put the chicken in a deep pot with the vegetables, bay leaf, sea salt and black pepper. Add enough water just to cover the chicken legs, leaving most of the breast uncovered. Bring to the boil, cover the pan and simmer for about 1 hour 20 minutes or until the chicken meat is cooked through. Transfer the chicken to a large, deep bowl. Pour in all the stock and vegetables, cover and leave in a cool place until cold. Then chill overnight.

2. Next day lift the chicken from the stock. Cut off the breast fillets in 2 large pieces, with the skin still attached. Wrap them in clingfilm until shortly before serving so that they don't dry out. Put the rest of the chicken back in the stock and boil again for 1½ hours to make a truly delicious consommé.

3. Before assembling the salad, cover the sun-dried tomatoes with boiling water and leave to stand for 5 minutes; then drain them, pat dry and cut in broad strips. Divide the chicken breast into small neat pieces, using a knife and fingers. Pile the salad leaves in a large dish and scatter the sliced cucumber, sun-dried tomatoes and chilli rings over all. Mix the dressing ingredients together and pour most of the dressing over the salad. Toss well, then lay the chicken fillets over the top and moisten them with the rest of the dressing. Serve immediately.

herb and spice information: bay leaves p27; pepper p79; rocket p24; chillies p56

spiced chicken salad

spicy salad

375 g (12 oz) tomatoes, skinned
and chopped

½ cucumber, chopped

½ large mild onion, chopped

1 bunch watercress, cut into
small sprigs

Dressing:

5 tablespoons olive oil

2 tablespoons lemon juice

⅛ teaspoon chilli powder or
cayenne, or a dash of Tabasco sauce

Serves 4

*In Egypt a spicy mixed salad is made by adding
shatah, a pounded chilli pepper, to the salad dressing.
The same effect can be achieved by using chilli
powder, cayenne or Tabasco sauce.*

1. Mix the chopped tomatoes, cucumber and onion
with the sprigs of watercress in a serving bowl.

2. For the dressing, mix the oil and lemon juice,
adding the chilli powder, cayenne or Tabasco sauce
to taste. Pour over the salad and mix thoroughly.

Note: This salad is best served alone or as a part of a
mixed hors-d'oeuvre, rather than as an
accompaniment to a main dish.

herb and spice information: watercress p32; chillies (powder) p56; cayenne p55

chocolate cakes
with strawberries and mint

75 g (3 oz) butter, part-melted, plus a little for greasing

125 g (4 oz) plain dark chocolate, such as Chocolat Menier, broken into small pieces

2 tablespoons plain flour, sifted

125 g (4 oz) caster sugar

3 eggs, separated

Filling:

200 g (7 oz) strawberries, chopped

1 heaped tablespoon chopped mint

250 ml (8 fl oz) double cream, lightly whipped

Serves 8

1. Heat the oven to 180°C (350°F), Gas Mark 4. Prepare 8 shallow round baking tins with flat bottoms, about 10 cm (4 inches) in diameter and 1.5 cm (¾ inch) deep. Grease the baking tins with butter, then line the bottoms with circles of buttered greaseproof paper.

2. Put the chocolate into a fairly large ovenproof bowl and place in the oven until the chocolate has just melted, about 5–10 minutes. Remove from the oven (but keep the oven at the same temperature) and leave to cool for 5 minutes. Then add the part-melted butter gradually, beating with a wooden spoon until it is combined with the chocolate. Stir in the flour and sugar. Beat the egg yolks briefly and stir into the chocolate mixture.

3. Whisk the egg whites until stiff and use a metal spoon to fold them into the mixture. Spoon into the tins to fill them by just over half. Bake for 15 minutes, until risen and set. Then leave to cool.

4. When the cakes have just cooled, the puffy crust that has formed on the top of the cakes, which is cracked and split, can be removed. Lift off as much as you can, one cake at a time. Put 2 tablespoons of chopped strawberries in the centre of each cake. Sprinkle with ½ teaspoon chopped mint, then spoon the lightly whipped cream over it. Replace the chocolate crust and then chill in the refrigerator until you are ready to serve.

Note: The cakes may be made a day in advance, then filled a short while before serving, but the crust will be hard to lift off if the cakes have been allowed to stand overnight. It is better to remove it soon after baking and reserve it separately.

herb and spice information: mint p31

honey & ginger
ice cream

This is made with a mixture of double cream and natural yogurt and is therefore less rich than an ice made purely with cream.

300 ml (½ pint) semi-skimmed milk

1 vanilla pod, halved and split into 4 pieces

2 eggs

2 egg yolks

1 tablespoon vanilla sugar or caster sugar

2 tablespoons clear aromatic honey, such as Greek or Mexican

2 tablespoons ginger syrup (from a jar of preserved stem ginger)

150 ml (¼ pint) mild natural yogurt

150 ml (¼ pint) double cream, partly whipped

3 tablespoons chopped preserved stem ginger

Serves 6

1. Put the milk in a small pan with the vanilla pod, including the seeds. Bring slowly to the boil, remove from the heat and let stand, covered, for 20–30 minutes. Beat the eggs and egg yolks together in a heatproof bowl using an electric mixer. Add the sugar gradually, continuing to beat until the mixture is pale and creamy. Reheat the milk with the honey and ginger syrup.

2. When almost boiling remove the vanilla pod (rinse, dry and keep to flavour a jar of vanilla sugar). Pour the milk on to the eggs and continue beating. Stand the bowl over a pan of simmering water and stir constantly until the mixture has slightly thickened. This may take 8–10 minutes. Remove from the heat. Stand the bowl in a sink half full of cold water to cool. Stir occasionally to prevent a skin from forming.

3. When the mixture has cooled almost to room temperature, pour it into a liquidizer or food processor. Add the yogurt and semi-whipped cream and blend briefly. Pour into an ice cream machine and freeze, following the maker's instructions, adding the chopped ginger halfway through the freezing time.

4. Alternatively, pour the mixture into a metal freezer container and place in the freezer. Freeze until part-frozen – 2–3 hours, depending on the shape and type of the container and the freezer. Stir with a metal spoon every hour or so and add the chopped ginger after 1½ hours. This method, although slow, produces a perfectly good ice cream even though it lacks the silky-smooth quality of the machine-made product.

herb and spice information: ginger p89

small iced cakes
with flowers

Crystallized flowers for the decoration must be prepared in advance. If making these seems too fiddly, freshly picked flowers or edible leaves, like nasturtiums, may be used instead. Failing flowers or edible leaves, small berries or currants may be used: red or white currants, blueberries and so on. Lemon juice may be substituted for the elderflower cordial. To half-melt the butter you need to heat it gently, until it is quite softened but not melted.

2 eggs

about 150 g (5 oz) vanilla sugar or caster sugar

about 150 g (5 oz) butter, part-melted

about 60 g (2½ oz) plain flour, sifted

about 60 g (2½ oz) ground almonds

Elderflower Icing:

175 g (6 oz) icing sugar

about 3 tablespoons elder-flower cordial

a few small crystallized flowers, to decorate

Makes about 16

1. Weigh the eggs together in their shells and note the weight – it should be about 150 g (5 oz), depending on the size of eggs. Then weigh the same quantity each of sugar and butter. The combined weight of flour and ground almonds should also be the same as that of the eggs.

2. In a large bowl, beat the eggs, then gradually add the sugar, continuing to beat until the mixture is very pale and thick. Then fold in the flour and ground almonds, and stir in the part-melted butter until well-combined. Spoon into well-buttered, small round cake tins measuring roughly 6 cm (2½ inches) across and 2.5 cm (1 inch) deep. Bake in a preheated oven, 180°C (350°F), Gas Mark 4, for 15–20 minutes, until risen and light golden brown with darker edges.

3. Leave the cakes to cool in the tins for 10–15 minutes, then place them on a wire rack. When they have completely cooled, prepare them for icing: if they have risen into a dome shape, level them by cutting off the central tip.

4. For the icing, sift the icing sugar into a bowl. Warm the elderflower cordial and stir it into the sugar, beating hard until absolutely smooth. Spread the icing over the little cakes and leave to set. Decorate with crystallized flowers.

ginger hats
with ginger sauce

75 g (3 oz) plain flour

75 g (3 oz) self-raising flour

½ tablespoon ground ginger

¼ teaspoon ground allspice

125 g (4 oz) soft brown sugar

4 tablespoons treacle

4 tablespoons golden syrup

125 g (4 oz) butter

2 eggs, beaten

Serves 6

These little ginger cakes used to be served cold at teatime in English country houses between the wars. I like to serve them hot, as a pudding with Ginger Sauce (see page 191).

1. Butter 6 muffin tins, each about 125 ml (4 fl oz) capacity. Sift the flours and spices into a large bowl, then mix in the brown sugar.

2. Warm the treacle, syrup and butter in a small pan. When the butter has just melted, stir the mixture into the dry ingredients, then mix in the eggs.

3. Turn into the tins and bake in a preheated oven, 180°C (350°F), Gas Mark 4, for 20–25 minutes. Allow to cool in the tins for about 20 minutes before serving with a sauce or or lightly whipped cream.

spiced fruit salad

A friend and colleague, Sybil Kapoor, gave me this recipe, showing how spices can subtly enhance the flavour of fresh fruit. The choice of fruit can be altered to suit the time of year.

4 ripe peaches, peeled stoned and sliced

4 figs, each cut into 8

250 g (8 oz) blueberries

crème fraîche, to serve

Spiced Syrup:

300 ml (½ pint) water

125 g (4 oz) caster sugar

pared rind and juice of 1 lemon

3 star anise

6 black peppercorns

6 green cardamoms

1 vanilla pod

Serves 4

1. First prepare the spiced syrup. Place the water, sugar, lemon rind and spices in a saucepan over moderate heat. Stir to dissolve the sugar before bringing the syrup to the boil. Simmer gently for 10 minutes, then remove from the heat. Add the lemon juice and leave to cool. The longer the spices are left in the syrup, the spicier the syrup will become.

2. Strain the syrup, or remove the lemon rind, and pour the syrup, with or without the spices, into a bowl. Add the sliced peaches, cut figs and blueberries. Chill and serve with crème fraîche.

Note: Half the fun of spiced fruit salads is varying the spices to taste. Coriander seeds can replace the star anise and/or a small cinnamon stick can be used instead of the vanilla pod. These subtle flavours can be enhanced by using an orange instead of lemon. I often add 2–4 tablespoons tamarind syrup to the cooling spiced syrup. Tamarind syrup is simple to make: break 175 g (6 oz) compressed tamarind into pieces and place in a saucepan with 1.2 litres (2 pints) water. Boil for about 20 minutes, until reduced by half, then strain. Dissolve 375 g (12 oz) sugar in the liquid and strain again. Store in an airtight jar in the refrigerator.

strawberries
with black pepper

An unusual but surprisingly good combination, especially when made with the juice of blood oranges, this makes a refreshing dessert at the end of a fairly elaborate dinner. It also makes a delicious breakfast for those who like to avoid sweet dishes at the start of the day.

500 g (1 lb) strawberries, hulled and thickly sliced

6 tablespoons freshly squeezed juice of blood oranges, when available, or ordinary oranges

black pepper

Serves 4

1. Lay the sliced strawberries on individual dishes or on a single flat dish. Pour the orange juice on top and grind a light sprinkling of black pepper over them.

Note: For a breakfast dish for 1 person, I allow 175 g (6 oz) strawberries.

herb and spice information: pepper p79

cucumber and yogurt sauce

150 ml (¼ pint) natural yogurt

½ cucumber, peeled and
coarsely grated

1 garlic clove, crushed

1½ tablespoons chopped fresh mint
or 1½ teaspoons dried mint

salt and white pepper

Serves 3 to 4

This sauce is delicious with roast lamb, meatballs or grilled chicken

1. Put the yogurt in a liquidizer or food processor. Using your hands, squeeze out any excess liquid from the grated cucumber, then add the cucumber to the yogurt with the crushed garlic, salt and pepper. Process briefly, just until blended. Alternatively, beat the yogurt by hand until smooth, then fold in the cucumber and garlic and mix well, adding salt and pepper to taste.

2. Stir in most of the mint, reserving a little for garnish. Turn the sauce into a bowl and scatter the rest of the mint over the top. Chill until ready to serve.

herb and spice information: garlic p11; mint p31

watercress sauce

Serve this sauce with poached fish, steamed or poached chicken, hard-boiled eggs or vegetables.

1. Pull the leaves off the watercress and set aside. Chop the stalks roughly and put in a pan with the stock. Bring to the boil slowly, cover and simmer for 20 minutes. Strain, then discard stalks and measure the stock: you should have about 300 ml (½ pint); if necessary, make it up to this amount with extra stock or water.

2. Melt the butter in a saucepan. Add the flour and cook for 1 minute, stirring. Gradually pour in the hot watercress stock, stirring continuously, and bring to the boil. Simmer for 3 minutes.

3. Purée the reserved watercress leaves with the cream in a liquidizer or food processor and add to the sauce. Reheat gently, stirring, but do not boil. Add salt and pepper to taste. Serve hot.

Note: For a cold sauce, make as above, then allow to cool. Process in a liquidizer or food processor once more, adding 125 ml (4 fl oz) natural yogurt.

1 bunch watercress

450 ml (¾ pint) fish or chicken stock

40 g (1½ oz) butter

2 tablespoons plain flour

300 ml (½ pint) single cream

salt and black pepper

Serves 4 to 5

herb sauce

75 ml (3 fl oz) natural yogurt

75 ml (3 fl oz) fromage frais

3 tablespoons chopped chervil,
tarragon or dill

25 g (1 oz) butter

1 tablespoon plain flour

175 ml (6 fl oz) fish or
chicken stock, heated

1 teaspoon Dijon mustard

salt and black pepper

Serves 4

*This light herb sauce is good with poached fish or
chicken, hard-boiled eggs, or vegetables.*

1. Blend the yogurt and fromage frais in a liquidizer
or food processor with the chopped herbs.
Alternatively, stir these ingredients together by hand.

2. Melt the butter in a saucepan over a low heat, add
the flour and cook for 1 minute, stirring. Gradually
pour in the heated fish or chicken stock, stirring
continuously. Add the mustard, salt and pepper, and
bring to the boil. Simmer for 3 minutes, stirring
occasionally, then remove from the heat. Stir the
herb mixture into the sauce and reheat very gently,
keeping well below boiling point as the yogurt and
fromage frais curdle easily. Serve soon after making.

herb and spice information: chervil p15; tarragon p17; dill p13; mustard seeds p83

mayonnaise

Homemade mayonnaise is not only delicious in its own right, for serving with shellfish, hard-boiled eggs, cold fish, chicken or warm vegetables, it also provides an admirable vehicle for using chopped fresh herbs and garlic.

Do not use the best extra virgin olive oil for making mayonnaise, for it will be too rich, heavy and cloying. If desired, a couple of spoonfuls of extra virgin olive oil may be added at the end for flavour.

1. Stand a large heavy bowl with a firm base on a damp cloth so it will not slip. Have the light olive oil in a jug and the vinegar and lemon juice to hand.

2 egg yolks

a pinch of sea salt

300 ml (½ pint) light olive oil, or olive oil and sunflower oil mixed in equal parts

1½ tablespoons white wine vinegar

1½ tablespoons lemon juice

2 tablespoons extra virgin olive oil (optional)

2. Place the egg yolks in the bowl, add the salt and beat lightly with a wooden spoon. Using an electric mixer or a balloon whisk, add the oil very slowly indeed, almost literally drop by drop to begin with, and beat continuously until the mixture begins to thicken and the eggs become pale in colour. If making mayonnaise for the first time, it may be helpful to drip the oil from a large spoon at the very beginning of the process.

3. When about half the oil has been incorporated drop by drop, you may start to add it more quickly, in a thin stream. Stop adding oil occasionally and continue beating to ensure that all the oil has been absorbed. If the mixture becomes too thick, add half the vinegar or lemon juice. When all the oil is incorporated, stir in the remaining vinegar and lemon juice. Slowly mix the extra virgin olive oil, if using.

Note: Chilli mayonnaise is a delicious adaptation of the basic mayonnaise recipe. First make the mayonnaise as above. Place 1–2 teaspoons chilli powder in a large metal spoon and hold it over a gentle heat for a few seconds, moving it about and taking care not to let the chilli powder change colour. Cool slightly, then stir into the mayonnaise.

rocket pesto

125 g (4 oz) rocket leaves, (without stalks), torn in pieces

1 garlic clove, crushed

50 g (2 oz) pine nuts

50 g (2 oz) freshly grated Parmesan cheese

a pinch of sea salt

75 ml (3 fl oz) extra virgin olive oil

Makes about 300 ml (½ pint)

The true pesto is, of course, made with basil, but alternative versions can be made with other herbs. Here rocket is used; you might also want to try coriander. This pesto is perfect with pasta, gnocchi boiled potatoes and minestrone-type soups.

1. Put the rocket in a food processor with the garlic, pine nuts, Parmesan and salt. Process until blended, stopping to scrape the ingredients down from the sides once or twice. Then process again, adding the olive oil slowly through the lid. Alternatively, chop the rocket and pine nuts finely, then pound in a mortar with the garlic, Parmesan and salt. Then add the oil gradually, beating it in with a wooden spoon.

2. Once made, turn the pesto into a small bowl, cover with clingfilm and chill until needed. It will keep for several days in the refrigerator or for weeks in a suitable container in the freezer.

Note: For a classic pesto, as made in Genoa, substitute basil (leaves only) for the rocket and reduce the pine nuts by half. If possible, use half Sardo (a hard cheese from Sardinia) and half Parmesan.

herb and spice information: rocket p24; garlic p11

chilli sauce

25 g (1 oz) butter

2 tablespoons sunflower oil

1 small onion, chopped

425 g (14 oz) can chopped tomatoes

½ bay leaf

½ teaspoon sugar

1 red pepper

1 red chilli, deseeded and finely chopped

a dash of Tabasco (optional)

3 tablespoons chopped coriander leaves

salt and black pepper

Serves 4 to 5

This spicy sauce complements fish cakes, grilled chicken or hamburgers.

1. Heat the butter with half the oil in a frying pan and cook the onion gently until it starts to colour. Add the tomatoes, with their juice, and heat, stirring. Add the half bay leaf, sugar and salt and pepper. Simmer, uncovered, for about 15 minutes, or until thick.

2. Meanwhile, grill the red pepper until the skin has blackened, then scrape off the skin. Discard the stalk, seeds and pith, and cut the pepper into little strips. Heat the remaining oil in a small frying pan and cook the chilli for 1 minute, then add the grilled pepper strips and cook for 1 minute more, stirring constantly.

3. Add the pepper and chilli to the tomatoes and mix well. Simmer together for a moment or two, then remove the bay leaf from the sauce and turn off the heat. Add a dash of Tabasco, if you wish, then stir in the coriander and leave to cool.

4. Purée the sauce briefly in a blender or food processor, or rub it through a coarse food mill, then cover and chill overnight. Reheat the sauce gently to serve, but do not allow to boil.

harissa

Harissa comes from Tunisia, where it is invariably served with couscous. Harissa is also found in Morocco, Libya and Algeria. It is very hot indeed, and rivals the Indonesian sambal oelek in strength. Its main ingredient is puréed dried red chillies, combined with coriander, caraway and garlic. It can also be bought quite easily in small cans and tubes. Alternatively, Hot Sauce II (see page 188) can be used instead of harissa.

1. Cover the dried chillies in tepid water and leave to soak for 3–4 minutes. Drain the chillies, then chop them very finely and pound them in a mortar. Add the garlic and sea salt and continue to pound until reduced to a pulp.

2. Add the caraway seeds and pound again. When thoroughly blended, pack the sauce into a tiny jar and cover the surface with the olive oil. Seal tightly and store in the refrigerator.

Note: For a smooth sauce, grind the caraway seeds to a powder on their own, before adding them to the chilli paste.

50 g (2 oz) dried chillies, split and deseeded

25 g (1 oz) garlic, chopped

5 g (¼ oz) sea salt

25 g (1 oz) caraway seeds

1–1½ tablespoons olive oil

Makes 150 g (5 oz)

herb and spice information: chillies p56; garlic p11; caraway seeds p57

rouille

10 g (⅓ oz) dry white bread

3 tablespoons fish stock, fish soup or milk

2 dried chillies, deseeded and finely chopped

2 garlic cloves, finely chopped

½ teaspoon sea salt

¼ teaspoon saffron threads

1 egg yolk (optional)

3 tablespoons extra virgin olive oil

1 tablespoon fish soup

Serves 6

This pungent Provençal sauce is the essential accompaniment to Mediterranean fish soups, made with a mixture of fish and spiced with saffron, orange rind and fennel (see Fish Soup with Fennel, page 101). Rouille may be spread on slices of French bread that have been dried in a low oven and floated in the soup, or it may simply be stirred into the hot soup.

1. Soak the bread in the stock, soup or milk for 5 minutes, then squeeze dry. Pound the chillies, garlic, salt and saffron in a mortar. Add the egg yolk, if using, and pound again. Add the soaked bread and pound until blended to a paste.

2. Add the oil drop by drop, stirring, as if making mayonnaise. When all the oil is incorporated, stir in 1 tablespoon of the fish soup to thin the rouille slightly. Transfer to a small bowl and serve.

Note: I usually add an egg yolk, as this makes the sauce more unctuous, as well as slightly more robust and less likely to separate. If you prefer, you may make the sauce without the egg yolk; however, if the mixture begins to separate, start again by breaking an egg yolk into a clean bowl and gradually stirring the split sauce, drop by drop, into it.

hot sauce I and II

Version I

½ teaspoon Harissa (see page 186)

1 tablespoon tomato purée

2 tablespoons hot chicken, meat, fish or vegetable stock

Serves 4 to 6

The first Hot Sauce is made with Harissa (see page 186), the ultra-hot paste based on chilli peppers and used throughout the Arab countries of northern Africa. It can be made at home or bought fairly easily.

1. Mix the harissa with the tomato purée in a small bowl. Stir in the hot stock, which should be taken from the dish for which the sauce is an accompaniment – usually a lamb, chicken or vegetable stew served with couscous. Pour into a tiny dish and serve.

Version II

1 teaspoon ground cumin

1 teaspoon ground coriander

½ teaspoon chilli powder

2 tablespoons tomato purée

2 tablespoons hot chicken, meat, fish or vegetable stock

Serves 4 to 6

This is a quick and easy substitute for the real thing, to be made when you do not have any harissa, nor the inclination to make some.

1. Mix the ground cumin, ground coriander and chilli powder and stir them into the tomato purée. Add the hot stock, taken from the dish the sauce is to accompany, and pour into a small serving dish.

herb and spice information: cumin seeds (ground) p62; coriander seeds (ground) p60; chillies (powder) p56

green curry paste

1 teaspoon coriander seeds

1 teaspoon caraway seeds

10 black peppercorns

½ teaspoon ground nutmeg

½ teaspoon ground cloves

10 large green chillies, deseeded and chopped

2 tablespoons chopped shallot

2 tablespoons chopped garlic

1 tablespoon grated galangal or fresh root ginger

2 stalks lemon grass, crushed and chopped

pared rind of 2 lemons, chopped

2 teaspoons sea salt

4 tablespoons sunflower oil

Makes about 100 g (3½ oz), enough for about 4 curries

In Thailand curries are made mostly with pastes made from a complex combination of fresh and dried herbs and freshly ground spices. This green curry paste uses large quantities of green chillies, fresh lemon grass and limes, and is especially suited to fish and chicken dishes.

1. Pound the coriander, caraway seeds and peppercorns in a mortar until crushed. Alternatively, grind the spices in an electric spice mill or coffee grinder. Transfer the crushed spices to a food processor.

2. Add all the other ingredients and process the mixture to a rough paste. Pack the paste into a screw-top jar and store in the refrigerator. The paste will keep for 4–6 weeks in an airtight jar in the refrigerator.

herb and spice information: coriander seeds p60; caraway seeds p57; pepper p79; nutmeg p73; cloves p65; chillies p56; garlic p11; galangal p71; ginger p89; lemon grass p23

189

smoky salsa

1–2 smoked dried chillies, halved and deseeded

300 g (10 oz) tomatoes

1 red pepper

1 bunch spring onions, sliced

2 tablespoons lime juice

2 tablespoons chopped coriander leaves

sea salt and black pepper

Makes 300 ml (½ pint); to serve 6

This tasty sauce complements all manner of bland foods, such as shellfish, fishcakes, egg croquettes and vegetable fritters.

1. Put the dried chilli(es) in a small bowl and cover with 4 tablespoons boiling water, then leave to soak for 20 minutes. Drain the chillies, reserving the water and purée them in a small blender or coffee mill with half the soaking water.

2. Thread the tomatoes and the pepper on skewers and grill them, turning frequently, until charred all over. The tomatoes will take just a few minutes, the pepper slightly longer. Leave to cool, then remove the skins. Discard the seeds from the pepper and cut it and the tomatoes into chunks. Put them into a food processor with the spring onions, chilli purée, sea salt and black pepper. Process until blended into a coarse purée.

3. Turn the salsa into a bowl and stir in the lime juice and chopped coriander leaves. Serve at room temperature or chilled.

herb and spice information: chillies p56; spring onions p10; coriander leaves p22

ginger sauce

450 ml (¾ pint) milk

½ vanilla pod, split

3 egg yolks

2½ tablespoons vanilla sugar or caster sugar

½ tablespoon ground ginger

2 teaspoons syrup from a jar of preserved stem ginger (optional)

1½–2 tablespoons finely chopped preserved stem ginger (optional)

Serves 4 to 6

This is a delicious sauce for serving with baked or steamed sponges, apple puddings or vanilla ice cream. The preserved ginger is not essential, but it adds a subtle and complex flavour to the sauce.

1. Pour the milk into a pan. Scrape the seeds from the vanilla pod into the milk and then add the pod. Warm the milk slowly until it is about to boil. Turn off the heat and cover, then leave to infuse for 30 minutes. Reheat gently and remove the pod.

2. Put the egg yolks in a large heatproof bowl. Add the sugar and ground ginger, and beat with an electric mixer or a balloon whisk. When the milk is about to boil for the second time, strain it and pour it on to the egg yolks, continuing to beat.

3. Stand the bowl over a saucepan half full of simmering water and stir briskly with a wooden spoon until the sauce starts to thicken. This may take as long as 8 minutes. When it has thickened enough to coat the back of the spoon, remove the bowl from the pan and stand it in a sink half full of cold water.

4. Cool the sauce until it is lukewarm. Stir occasionally to prevent a skin from forming. Add the ginger syrup and chopped ginger, if using, then process briefly in a blender or food processor. Serve warm with hot or cold puddings, or ice cream.

parsley butter

250 g (8 oz) butter, at room temperature

2 garlic cloves, crushed

6 tablespoons chopped flat-leaf parsley

2 tablespoons lemon juice

sea salt and black pepper

Serves 8

1. Cream the butter in a food processor, adding the garlic, parsley, lemon juice, salt and pepper. Alternatively, cream the butter by hand, then add the other ingredients and mix thoroughly. Chill for 30 minutes, or until firm. Form into a roll and cut in half. Wrap each half in clingfilm or foil and chill until required or freeze.

Note: This is sometimes called maître d'hôtel butter. To serve with fish, replace the crushed garlic with ½ tablespoon finely chopped shallot.

coriander butter

Use coriander leaves instead of parsley. Serve with grilled steaks, burgers, tomatoes or mushrooms. Omit the garlic if serving with fish.

dill butter

Use dill instead of parsley and omit the garlic. Serve with poached trout, boiled asparagus, grilled tomatoes or new potatoes.

mixed herb butter

Use 1 tablespoon each of chervil, chives, dill, mint, tarragon and salad burnet instead of the parsley. Add 1 tablespoon finely chopped shallot instead of the garlic. Serve with grilled fish, meat or vegetables.

herb and spice information: coriander leaves p22; dill p13; chervil p15; chives p12; mint p31; tarragon p17; salad burnet p38

dill pickles

1 kg (2 lb) gherkins or small
cucumbers, or halved
cucumbers cut in wedges

2 garlic cloves, thinly sliced

12 large sprigs dill, including
flowers if possible

3 bay leaves

Pickle:

750 ml (1¼ pints) water

250 ml (8 fl oz) vinegar

25 g (1 oz) sea salt

12 black peppercorns

12 allspice berries

Makes 1 kg (2 lb)

These traditional accompaniments to salt beef and pastrami sandwiches are best made in midsummer, when gherkins are available and dill is plentiful. This recipe really needs thick stalks and flower heads as well as leaves, so homegrown dill is infinitely better than that sold in shops and supermarkets.

1. Wash a 1 kg (2 lb) glass preserving jar and its lid in sterilizing solution (the type used for baby feeding equipment), then place upside down on an oven rack. Turn the oven to 120°C (250°F), Gas Mark ½, and leave the jar for 15 minutes. Then turn off the heat, leaving the jar in the oven. It should still be warm when you are filling it.

2. Pack the washed gherkins (or small cucumbers or wedges) into the jar, adding the garlic, dill and bay leaves. Put all the ingredients for the pickle into a pan and boil for 3 minutes, then leave to cool before pouring over the gherkins.

3. Cool, then close the jar tightly. Keep for at least 2 weeks before eating. Once opened, the pickles should be kept in the refrigerator.

herb and spice information: garlic p11; dill p13; bay leaves p27; pepper p79; allspice p76

mint chutney

500 g (1 lb) cooking apples,
peeled, cored and chopped

250 g (8 oz) onions,
coarsely chopped

2 garlic cloves, finely chopped

1 yellow pepper, cored,
deseeded and chopped

450 ml (¾ pint) white wine vinegar

25 g (1 oz) fresh root ginger, bruised

250 g (8 oz) moist brown sugar

1 teaspoon coriander seeds

4 black peppercorns

4 allspice berries

½ tablespoon sea salt

4 tablespoons chopped mint

Makes about 1 litre (1¾ pints)

1. Prepare your preserving jars. Preheat the oven to 120°C (250°F), Gas Mark ½. Wash glass preserving jars and their lids in sterilizing solution (the type used for baby feeding equipment), then place upside down on an oven rack and leave for 15 minutes. Then turn off the heat, leaving the jars in the oven. They should still be hot or warm as you are filling them.

2. Put the apples, onions, garlic and yellow pepper into a heavy-based pan with the vinegar. Bring slowly to the boil and simmer until soft, about 30 minutes. Tie the ginger in a piece of muslin and add to the pan with the sugar, coriander seeds, peppercorns, allspice and salt. Heat the mixture gently until the sugar has dissolved, then simmer until thick; this may take up to 1 hour.

3. Discard the the ginger and stir in the chopped mint. Spoon the chutney into warm sterilized jars and leave to cool. Then close the jars tightly, wipe them with a damp cloth and label them clearly.

4. To serve, spoon some chutney into a bowl and sprinkle some freshly chopped mint on top. It is excellent with rye bread and Cheddar cheese.

Note: To make coriander chutney, use chopped fresh coriander instead of mint.

b and spice information: garlic p11; ginger p89; coriander seeds p22; pepper p79; allspice p76;
t p31

mango relish

2 mangoes, slightly under-ripe, peeled and chopped

5 spring onions, white parts only, sliced

1 green chilli, deseeded and finely chopped

5 cm (2 inch) piece fresh root ginger, peeled and grated

4 tablespoons lime juice

2 tablespoons chopped coriander leaves

sea salt and black pepper

1. Mix all the ingredients in a food processor and chop them together briefly until combined, but still coarse in texture. Alternatively, place all the ingredients in a bowl and use a hand-held blender to chop them. Serve at room temperature with curries.

Serves 4

herb and spice information: spring onions p10; chillies p56; ginger p89; coriander leaves p22

pickled kumquats

Autumn is the time to pickle kumquats, when they are readily available in the shops. Serve with cold meat and game.

1. Put the kumquats in a pan and cover with water. Bring to the boil, reduce the heat and cook steadily for about 35 minutes or until the kumquats are soft when pierced with a skewer. Drain the kumquats.

500 g (1 lb) kumquats

500 g (l lb) sugar

450 ml (3⁄4 pint) red or white wine vinegar

5 cm (2 inch) stick cinnamon

6 cloves

Makes about 1 kg (2 lb)

2. Put the sugar in a clean pan and add the vinegar and spices. Bring to the boil and cook gently until the sugar has dissolved. Then add the kumquats and bring back to the boil. Simmer gently for 15 minutes, then cover and leave to stand overnight.

3. Bring the pickle back to the boil and simmer for another 15 minutes. Remove from the heat, lift out the fruit with a slotted spoon and pack it into preserving jars. Boil the syrup until it has reduced just enough to cover the kumquats and fill the jars. Pour the syrup over the kumquats and cover at once with airtight lids. Keep for 1 month before eating, if you can bear to.

Note: Because the kumquats are pickled in vinegar, the jars do not need to be sterilized and sealed as for bottled fruit in syrup. An airtight seal is all that is needed, otherwise the vinegar will evaporate.

yogurt drink
with rose petals

600 ml (1 pint) mild natural yogurt

3–4 tablespoons rose water

about 300 ml (½ pint) iced water

4 tablespoons caster sugar

8 rose petals, to decorate

Serves 2 to 3

This is a festive drink that might be served at a party in Turkey or India. These sweet versions of the lightly salted, mint-flavoured yogurt drinks are normally flavoured with rose water. If possible, use a few petals of a pink damask rose for a decoration.

1. Blend the yogurt in a liquidizer or food processor, or beat by hand until smooth. Add the rose water, iced water and sugar. Process or beat together, then taste for sweetness and check for consistency. Add more rose water as required, and more iced water if the mixture is still too thick. Finally, pour into tall glasses and scatter a few rose petals over the top.

herb and spice information: rose p39

Moroccan mint tea

This is a real mint tea, as made in North Africa, not just an infusion of mint, which is often called mint tea. It is very refreshing on a hot afternoon, or drunk after a meal instead of black coffee. In this context, it also serves as a digestive. If you cannot get Moroccan tea, the best alternatives are the China teas, such as chunmee, gunpowder or Temple of Heaven, or an ordinary green tea. Be sure to use spearmint, the common or garden mint, and not one of the scented varieties. Do not be tempted to omit the sugar, or even cut it down much more than I have done already.

1. Warm a small teapot of about 600 ml (1 pint) capacity, and put in the tea, sugar and mint leaves. Pour over enough boiling water to fill the pot and allow to brew for 5 minutes. Pour the tea from a height into 3–4 small glasses, and put a small sprig of mint in each one. Serve hot or warm.

1 tablespoon Moroccan or green tea

3–4 tablespoons sugar

24 large spearmint leaves

3–4 small sprigs spearmint

Serves 3 to 4

camomile tea

Serves 1

In former times camomile was made into an infusion and used as a final rinse when washing the hair, to keep fair hair light in colour. Nowadays it is used mainly in the form of camomile tea, also an infusion, to be drunk after dinner, instead of black coffee, as a light sedative. If using commercially produced camomile teabags, simply put 1 in a cup or mug and fill up with almost boiling water. Stand for 5 minutes, then remove the bag. If using the loose dried herb, place it in a ball or other wire mesh container. Failing that, the tea is best made in a small teapot, allowing 2 teaspoonfuls of dried camomile to 175 ml (6 fl oz) of nearly boiling water. Then strain the infusion into a cup. Fresh camomile may be used in the same way.

herb and spice information: camomile p14

linden-mint tea

1 teaspoon dried linden flowers

1 teaspoon dried mint

Serves 1

This is a delicious combination of dried herbs, very popular in France where it is called tilleul-menthe. *It is one of the best infusions for serving after dinner, as the linden flowers are a sedative, while the dried mint acts as a digestive. But be careful to use ordinary mint, not peppermint, which would not mix well with the linden.*

Put the loose herbs in a tea-infuser ball or other wire mesh container, and place in a fairly large cup or a small mug. Fill up with almost boiling water, then set aside to infuse for 5 minutes before removing the herbs.

herb and spice information: mint p31

fruit punch

A liquidizer is best for making this type of delicious, smooth concoction, but a food processor does the job adequately.

1. Put all the prepared fruit in a liquidizer or food processor with the orange juice or skimmed milk, roughly broken ice cubes and tamarind syrup, if using. Process at high speed until well blended and foamy. Pour into tumblers or glass bowls and serve at once.

500 g (1 lb) mixed fruit: bananas, melon, peaches, nectarines, plums, grapes and berries of all sorts, cut into chunks

100 ml (3½ fl oz) freshly squeezed orange juice or skimmed milk

3 ice cubes, broken

1 tablespoon tamarind syrup (see note on page 177; optional)

Note: This is almost too thick to drink, so you may prefer to eat it with a spoon. Whichever way you drink or eat it, it is utterly delicious.

Serves 3

herb and spice information: tamarind p84

spiced vodka

**1 bottle superlative vodka,
such as Absolut or Stolichnaya**

**3–5 small chillies,
red and green mixed**

**10 juniper berries,
very lightly crushed**

Makes 1 bottle.

Russian and Polish vodkas are often flavoured with different herbs, spices and fruit. This is one of the most unforgettable for the contrast between the heat of the chillies and the icy chill of the vodka, which is served just above freezing point. The recipe is simplicity itself.

1. Open the vodka bottle, slip in the chillies and the juniper berries and close tightly. Leave for 2–3 weeks before drinking.

2. If you have a freezer deep enough to hold the vodka bottle upright, you can create an ice waistcoat which looks spectacular. Stand the bottle in a container slightly larger than itself and fill the outer container with water, then stand the bottle and container in the freezer. When the water has frozen solid, slip off the outer container by immersing it briefly in warm water. Replace the vodka bottle, in its ice waistcoat, in the freezer. The vodka will not freeze, due to its high alcohol content; it will simply become slightly syrupy and all the more delicious.

index